Puppy Training in 7 Easy Steps

Everything You Need to Know to Raise the Perfect Dog

Sara Winters

© Copyright 2021 by Sara Winters. All right reserved.

The work contained herein has been produced with the intent to provide relevant knowledge and information on the topic described in the title for entertainment purposes only. While the author has gone to every extent to furnish up to date and true information, no claims can be made as to its accuracy or validity as the author has made no claims to be an expert on this topic. Notwithstanding, the reader is asked to do their own research and consult any subject matter experts they deem necessary to ensure the quality and accuracy of the material presented herein.

This statement is legally binding as deemed by the Committee of Publishers Association and the American Bar Association for the territory of the United States. Other jurisdictions may apply their own legal statutes. Any reproduction, transmission or copying of this material contained in this work without the express written consent of the copyright holder shall be deemed as a copyright violation as per the current legislation in force on the date of publishing and subsequent time thereafter. All additional works derived from this material may be claimed by the holder of this copyright.

The data, depictions, events, descriptions and all other information forthwith are considered to be true, fair and accurate unless the work is expressly described as a work of fiction. Regardless of the nature of this work, the Publisher is exempt from any responsibility of actions taken by the reader in conjunction with this work. The Publisher acknowledges that the reader acts of their own accord and releases the author and Publisher of any responsibility for the observance of tips, advice, counsel, strategies and techniques that may be offered in this volume.

Table of Contents

Introduction 5
Chapter 1: Getting Your Home Puppy Ready   7
    Preparing for Puppy 8
    So, You Think You Are Ready 12
Chapter 2: Common Puppy Issues, and How to Handle Them 25
    Using Play to Create Good Behaviors 25
    Stop Problem Behaviors Before They Begin 26
Chapter 3: Teaching Commands 36
    What Incentives Do I Need? 36
    Should They Master One Before Moving Onto Another Command? 37
    Should Things be Taught in a Certain Order? ... 37
    When Does Training Need to Start? 38
    Should Rewards be Given Each Time? 39
    Come 39
    Stay 41
    Touch 42
    Spin 43
    Leave It 44
    Place/On Your Bed 45
    Back 46
    Sit 47
    Lay Down 47
    Shake 48
Chapter 4: Seven Simple Steps to Housebreaking 49
Chapter 5: Crate Training 55
    Picking the Right Crate 56
    The Training Process 56
    Possible Problems 60
Chapter 6: Creating a Schedule 63
    Is a Schedule Necessary? 65
Chapter 7: Reading Your Dog 70
    Tail Wagging 70
    Raised Hackles 71

Posture..71
Facial Expressions..72
Eyes...73
Chapter 8: General Puppy Care.......... 80
Chapter 9: Socializing........................89
Socializing Them With Humans 94
Socializing Your Dog With New Dogs...............................96
Chapter 10: Puppy Training Mistakes .98
Conclusion 106

Introduction

The connection between dogs and humans is one of the strongest bonds we can experience. Even when they do things that we don't like, such as stealing food off of our plates. Dogs are probably one of the most loyal pets. The majority of dog owners will tell their dogs everything because they know that they can trust them to just be there and listen.

They always seem to be so happy. They get excited over some of the simplest things, and they know how to appreciate the little things in life. They are also like blankets with feet. Their cuddles are comforting and warm and can be one of the best things after a long stressful day.

They can also bring more exercise into your day. Even when you don't feel like going for a walk, you have to take your dog out for walks throughout the day. You'll feel grateful when you do take them out. On the subject of taking them for walks, they do all of their business outside. Cats require a litter box, but dogs don't. However, you will get used to having to carry around bags of poo.

They are also a source of happiness and love. Scientists have found that dogs release oxytocin when they interact with humans, which means that they actually do love us back. While a family member might not greet you with hugs and smiles when you get home from work, your dog will.
Dogs also have the power to make you laugh even when you don't feel like it. They want nothing more than to make you happy and to get you to give them belly rubs. Dogs are a great pet to have around. They can make your entire life better.

The only thing is, all of that love comes with a bit of a cost. You have to teach them how to not use the rug and any other trick or rule you would like them to obey. They will happily listen to you and do as you ask, as long as you teach them how to do so. That's what this book is here to help you with.

With the right information, you can teach your dog how you would like them to behave with love and understanding. In this book, we will go over things like getting your home ready for your new puppy, ten basic commands you should teach and how to teach them, and seven simple steps for housebreaking your puppy.

We'll go over many other things as well so that you are fully prepared for your new little bundle of joy. Having a dog should be fun, and this book will help make it so.

Before we begin, I would like to ask that if you find any part of this book helpful, a review on Amazon is always appreciated.

Chapter 1: Getting Your Home Puppy Ready

Getting a new member of the family is both stressful and exciting. The best method of keeping everybody happy and healthy is to be prepared and organized before you ever bring a new puppy home. Many people will spend months getting ready for a new baby, and these same people will grab a puppy and bring it home without ever thinking about it or getting their home ready. It isn't any wonder why they are constantly playing "catch-up" for possibly weeks, months, and years or they might even get rid of the small defenseless little puppy as they try to fix all the mistakes they made during the puppy's first few months.

Not having baby gates, a puppy pen, or a crate on the very first day will cause many housetraining mistakes. This could set back your housetraining efforts by days, weeks, and possibly months because your puppy is going to pee or poop anywhere they can still smell where they had an accident.

A good puppy owner has to put a lot of thought into bringing a puppy home. As a young child, I had asked for a puppy, and my parents gave me a leash, dog bowl, and gift certificate for Christmas instead of just buying me the Collie I had wanted for several years. This gave us time to get the house ready for the new "baby." It also gave us the opportunity to bring the baby into a structured home.

You might be wondering if your home needs to be "puppy-proofed," and the answer is yes. Getting a new puppy is almost the same as bringing home a new baby. Do you have all the supplies you need that the new puppy won't be able to live without? Does everybody in your house know the routine and rules? If not, we're here to help.

This chapter will help you create a comforting and safe environment for your new puppy. It will also help you find the tools and products to help you take care of your new baby.

Preparing for Puppy

Before you think about bringing the new puppy home, you need to walk through and look at your home, your routines, and think about the things your puppy needs from the first day. This lets you assess your environment and make any changes, buy what you need, and create a list of rules for the family before your puppy comes home.

This will make the transition into your home a lot less stressful for both your puppy and yourself. Keep in mind that the puppy's entire world is being turned upside down, and this transition will be a lot easier if you are completely ready for this new addition. Here are some things you can do to get your life and home ready.

- Get The Children Ready

If you have young children, you need to introduce them to the puppy before you bring it home. If at all possible, have every family member see the new puppy before you adopt it. You can get your children excited about the new dog by reading books about the dog's breed to them. Book stores and libraries will have informative books that will talk about everything from house training to teaching them tricks.

Allow your children to pick out some of the supplies that you are going to need for the new puppy while explaining what they are for and the ways to use them correctly. It would be a good idea to teach the children about the routine you need to get the puppy used to and allow them to take part. This can help make sure your children know when the puppy needs to rest and when it can play.

You will need to teach them how to correctly handle the puppy. This also goes for new puppies or an adult dog you rescue from an animal shelter. Your children are going to need to know all the boundaries about approaching the new dog, playtime, and when the dog might need some along time. This can keep your children or new puppy from getting injured. It can also help your children be less intimidating by the new puppy.

- Your New Puppy Needs Its Own Space

Although it is wonderful and exciting to have a new puppy in your home, young puppies need lots of rest, so you need to be sure they have a space that is dedicated just for them. When you have shown them around their new home, begin with the spot where they are to use the bathroom and then show them where they can have some alone time.

This might be an extra room, blanket, bed, crate, or kennel. Just be sure that it is a place just for them where there aren't any other pets or people. This needs to be a comfortable place that could help them stop any destructive behaviors and quiet their anxiety.

- Buy Supplies

You need to make sure you purchase all the needed supplies before you bring the puppy home. Ask about their diet so you can buy the same food to keep their diet regulated for the first month you have them. After they have settled in, you can then decide if you would like to change their food.

The first two weeks are the most crucial. This means you need to have enough supplies to give them a constant routine and have enough activities to keep your new puppy happy.

- Get Your Home Puppy-Proofed

Puppies love adventures. They are going to explore their new environment. You need to make sure they will be safe. This means you might have to block off some areas of your home, such as stairs until they have practiced going up and down them, so they don't tumble down them. Baby gates are a great way to section off various parts of your home that you don't want the puppy exploring.

Decorations and plants might be dangerous for your puppy if they eat them. This means you have to move them up so the puppy can't reach them. Power cords can be extremely hazardous to puppies. You will need to tape down or cover any loose cords to keep your puppy from chewing them or getting tangled up in them. Every toy is not a dog toy. You need to make sure your children keep their toys away from the puppy's toys.

Puppies will explore using their mouth. If things fit into their mouths, then this is where it will go. You need to make sure you keep a close watch on them when they are outside or inside. Your own backyard could have some dangerous things. They could get into their mouth.

Natural chews are the best alternative to keep your puppy from chewing on the furniture or shoes. You need to have some options for your puppy that can distract them from chewing on things they shouldn't.

- Learn About Your Puppy

Find a book about your puppy's breed. Specific breeds will have different grooming requirements, exercise demands, temperaments, and personality characteristics. You will need to choose a breed that you feel drawn to and will suit your lifestyle.

Talk to the puppy's breeder, previous owner, or rescue shelter to learn more about your puppy's favorite games, habits, and routines. The more you can learn about your puppy, you will be able to make them safe and comfortable in your home.

This would be the best time to think about their diet. Begin by looking at all the options you have and figure out which ones would suit the puppy's breed better. You can look at an online pet store or your local pet store that has the things you want. They might even have some samples that you can try on your new puppy.

- Look At Your Situation

If you are going through some stressful times, NEVER bring a new puppy into it. Stressful times might include anything from lots of noise, a lot of people, or if you will be spending time away from home. All of these factors could put more stress on a situation that is already stressful for an animal.

If you have planned a vacation, have relatives visiting, going through renovations, or moving, wait until all these things are over before bringing the puppy home. Puppies are already going to be stressed out because they are getting taken away from their litter mates, and mom and a busy, noisy home could affect this transition badly.

Once you have your puppy home, it is best to take some time off work so you can spend as much time as possible with them to get them adjusted. This helps you bond with them while creating their routine within their first week.

- Get Ready to Travel With Puppy

Bringing a new puppy is extremely exciting. It might be easy to forget some supplies that you might need for your journey home. Here are some supplies that you need to have with you:

1. Paper towels and wipes for accidents
2. Water dish
3. Leash and collar
4. Bed or blanket
5. Carrier or crate

This is going to overwhelm your puppy. They might bark, cry, or sleep all the way home. Having these supplies will ensure you are ready for any possibilities.

The new puppy needs to be positioned in your lap. If you are driving, you need to either put the puppy in a carrier or crate or have someone else with you that can hold the puppy. Never let the puppy wander around your vehicle as they could get stuck between seats or get hurt on other things.

- Have a Vet

You need to take your new puppy to your vet of choice in the first week that you bring them home. You will need to schedule this appointment before you bring them home. The vet will look at your dog and make sure that they are eating, digesting their food, and growing properly.

If this is your first pet, you will need to do some research and find one that you trust. Ask friends who have pets what vet they use. Read reviews and talk to the breeder or previous owner to help you find a vet that they recommend. Most vets use traditional medicine, but some are getting into holistic or integrative practices. Just find a vet who will support your pet and give you honest advice.

So, You Think You Are Ready

The most important thing you can ask yourself before you bring your puppy home is… "Should I get a puppy?"

Getting a puppy isn't something that you need to do spontaneously or without planning properly. There are reasons why there are animals in rescues and shelters.

Before you finally commit to a new puppy, take time and think long and hard about it. Talk to your roommates, family, or anybody else who lives in your home, and be sure this is a good fit for everybody involved.

If you haven't taken the time to think about how a puppy will fit into your life, you need to know if you are absolutely ready to take on all the responsibilities of owning a pet both financially and emotionally; this chapter will help you make this decision.

Never get discouraged if it seems like your puppy is taking longer to adapt to their new environment than you thought it would. Puppies have special needs, traits, and personalities. So you have to plan for errors and trials as both you and your puppy get adjusted. You might have to try several routines, toys, and foods to give your puppy what they need.

- Puppy Food

What your puppy eats is the foundation of its health. Picking the right food is the first step to owning a new puppy. The kind of diet you choose is totally up to you. You need to be sure you know all the options out there before you make this choice:

1. Dehydrated
2. Freeze-dried
3. Raw
4. Wet food
5. Kibble or Dry food

It would be a great idea to get some food that your puppy is already eating so you don't disrupt their digestive systems. It doesn't matter if you keep them on it; it is best to keep any diet changes to a minimum until they have gotten comfortable in your home.

Getting used to a new home is extremely stressful enough for a puppy. Keeping them on the same food will decrease any digestive upsets until they get used to their new life.

If you are changing their diet, be sure you leave some of their old food to get them transitioned properly. You need to wait about one month before you make any large dietary changes unless you absolutely have to.

Once you are ready to make changes to their food, it would be best to replace their old food slowly with the new food over the course of seven to ten days. Begin by replacing about one-fourth of the old food with the new one and slowly increasing this amount over a week or so.

- Food Accessories and Storing Their Food

The right accessories could help get rid of all your safety concerns and the guesswork out of creating your puppy's routine. The right food storage is going to help you keep your puppy's food fresher while preventing contamination.

There are several ways to store various kinds of foods. Let's look at each one and find the best way to keep your puppy's food safe for them:

1. Dehydrated or freeze-dried foods could be kept in a refrigerator in air-tight containers for a couple of days. Ready-to-eat or unprepared foods are best to keep them stored in their original packages, and once opened, you can put them into freezer bags to keep them the freshest.
2. Keeping raw food has two things to think about defrosted and frozen. You can store frozen foods in their original packaging, but you will need to put them into freezer bags if you want to store them for a long time. When the food has been thawed, it needs to be kept in the refrigerator in air-tight containers. You

should only keep thawed, raw foods for three days in the fridge.
3. You have to put any opened wet food in the refrigerator. The kind of wet food is changing the way you can store it. Cans are the most convenient, and you can put a reusable lid on them before placing them in the refrigerator. These help keep moisture in and oxygen away from the food. If the wet food comes in tetra packs or pouches, it needs to be put into a glass, air-tight container to keep it fresh.
4. Dry dog food or kibble can be kept in its original package inside a container that is air-tight. The bags have been coated to help protect the food from getting contaminated or oxidizing. After the bags get opened, there isn't any way to reseal them. When you put the bag into an air-tight container, you are protecting and making sure the food stays fresher for a long time. This way will reduce the chances of bacteria building up inside the plastic container. This is the most affordable option.

Other than food storage, there are other tools that will be useful for you and will help keep meals easy to serve. Mats and scoops can help keep meals from getting messy. If you want to measure out the correct amount of food, you could get a scale.

- Food Dishes

If you look at pet food dishes either online or in a store, you are going to get bombarded with a lot of choices. You are going to see automatic, elevated, weighted, steel, ceramic, and plastic.

Plastic ones are the cheapest, but they have some drawbacks when compared to other materials. As we have established, puppies love to chew. Plastic bowls might be the cheapest, but to your puppy, they look like a chew toy. They are light, so it will be easy for your puppy to pick it up in their mouth and carry it around. They will have it destroyed in no time at all.

As the plastic begins to wear, bacteria will begin hiding in all the grooves and scratches. This bacteria could cause some digestive problems; this could cause small pimples on their chin. This will go away if you get rid of the source of bacteria. It would be best if you used metal, ceramic, or glass to steer clear of bacteria and acne.

If your puppy eats extremely fast, you might want to think about getting them a "slow-feed bowl." This helps regulate how quickly they eat. It keeps them from ingesting huge mouthfuls of food at one time.

- Fountains or Water Dishes

Just like the food dishes, you need to steer clear of plastic water dishes, too. Even if you clean their bowls daily and replace the water, plastic bowls need to be replaced quicker than glass, ceramic, or metal dishes.

Water bowls are the norm, and fountains do have some benefits for your puppy. Fountains are a great way to keep their water clean and cool. Fountains just need to be topped off either every other day or each day and changed out totally weekly.

If you do decide to just use a bowl, be sure your puppy will always have access to clean water. This could mean changing their water several times each day.

- Treats

Treats will make your life easier when it comes time to train your puppy. Find various health treats that your puppy will go crazy for to keep their attention while you train them. These rewards need to be meaty, smelly, chewy, or soft. Pups that love food might not even care about the type of treatment they are getting just, so they get something to eat.

Try to find treats that have ingredients like whole foods and are healthy. Be sure the treats are low-calorie and small enough so you can give them several during the training. When talking about training, the smaller the treat, the better.

You can tear soft treats up into smaller pieces, so they aren't actually eating too many. Any treat you use for training needs to be smaller than a normal piece of kibble. Other than treats, some other natural chews, such as dried fish skin or beef tendons, are great to give your pup something to chew on.

- Collar and Leashes

Before your puppy gets its first vaccines, you shouldn't let them interact too much with the outside world. You can get them used to walk on a leash immediately. The two things that you need to begin teaching them good walking manners are a collar and leash.

You can practice in your backyard or house so they will be used to the equipment when they get ready to explore. It is all going to depend on the puppy's breed, but they might grow quickly in 18 months, or they might not grow that much at all. It really doesn't matter. Just try to find some walking equipment that fits them well now but is adjustable, so they have room to grow. This will lessen how quickly you have to get new equipment.

Harnesses are great choices to teach your puppy not to pull on their leash while walking. Collars put a lot of stress on a puppy's fragile neck. This makes harnesses safer and gives you better control over your pup.

Collars are still an important accessory as they can hold their vaccination tags, licenses, and ID tags. It is also an easy way to grab onto your pet if an emergency arises. Try to find a collar that will be comfortable for them to wear all day long.

- Poop Bags

You can't ever be caught without having some poop bags with you. It doesn't matter if you think you are just going for a short walk or just going from your car into the store; you don't even know when your puppy is going to need to poop. It would be very smart to buy these in bulk.

You can find poop bags in various styles, so you get to pick the one that will work best for you. Many poop bags only come in one size, but you can find bigger ones if you are raising a bear.

Any eco-friendly pet owner loves finding biodegradable or recyclable poop bags. Who wouldn't want to pick up their dog's poop that is biodegradable with a poop bag that is biodegradable? Mother Earth will thank you.

For people who have sensitive noses and an easily queasy tummy, you may need to look for poop bags that are scented. These won't totally get rid of the smell, but they will soften it a lot. Just choose a scent that you know normally use inside your home since it will not be as pleasant for you from now on.

- Accessories

Everything can be an opportunity to train your puppy, so be sure you have all the right accessories and tools so you can be successful. If you use treats when training, you are going to need a treat pouch or bag so you can carry them with you when you are out and about with your puppy.

A clicker is another great training accessory that you can use by itself or with treats. You can attach your clicker to their leash or put it around your wrist, so it will always be handy.

If you are training your puppy in open spaces, a whistle might help you get your puppy's attention faster. You could get a silent one that won't be as abrasive to the people around you.

- ID Tags

Even if you don't ever let your puppy out of your sight, you need to be sure they are tagged. Having an ID tag on their collar will make it easier and safer for them to get back home if they do happen to run away or venture out on their own.

If you don't want all the jingling from numerous tags clanging together, you could get some silencers for their tags. These will cut down on the noise, but they keep the tags from rubbing together and getting rid of the engraving with time.

- Brush

You need to brush your puppy at the very least one time each week. It doesn't matter what breed they are either. If your puppy has long hair, you might need to brush them every other day. Brushing will reduce matting, shedding and will help stimulate their hair to grow healthier. Begin will a soft slicker brush and make sure it has plastic or rubber tips because this will be gentle on their skin that is very sensitive.

The earlier you begin brushing your puppy, the better off you will be. Try to have some treats handy when you brush them. Giving them treats will help them see brushing them as a positive experience and will make it easier to keep doing this as they get older,

If your pup is fluffy, especially if they are a breed that has an undercoat, you might want to find a de-shedding brush that you use on them once each week to keep the amount of dog hair to a minimum.

- Puppy Wipes and Tear-Free Shampoo

A puppy's skin is extremely sensitive. Bathing them too much or at a very young age could reduce all the natural oils on their skin that protect them. Try your best not to bathe a puppy that is under 12 weeks old.

Try to spot clean or use a natural wipe to clean them if they get messy. Just because you shouldn't bathe them, it doesn't mean they have to stink. If you absolutely have to give your puppy a bath, find a shampoo that is made from gentle and all-natural ingredients.

Make sure you pick a shampoo that is made just for dogs. Human shampoos have been made for skin pHs that are very different. Getting and using the wrong shampoo could dry your puppy's skin and coat, and it could cause some allergic reactions.

- Toothpaste and Toothbrush

Yes, they do make toothbrushes and toothpaste for puppies, and you need to get your puppy used to brush their teeth as quickly as you can. You need to try your best to brush your teeth each day. Having good brushing habits means a lower vet bill in their lifetime.

A small finger toothbrush is great for smaller mouths and will be easier for your puppy to handle. You can slowly switch to a normal puppy toothbrush with time.

Even if they hate brushing their teeth, keep introducing them to it. There isn't another way to take care of your puppy's teeth.

- Nail Clippers

Just like brushing your puppy's teeth, trimming their nails at an early age will help them get used to it, and they won't have any anxiety or fear about it. Puppies don't need to have their nails trimmed too often while they are young since their nails haven't grown out past the quick. You only need to clip off the tips.

Find some clippers that are comfortable for you to use and are suited for your puppy's nails. If you are comfortable, the grooming process will be easier, too. If your puppy is extremely young, clippers for cats might work easier when you are both learning.

As your puppy gets bigger, their nails will grow faster; you can begin cutting a back further just be conscious of their quick. If you aren't comfortable trimming your puppy's nails, you could think about using a nail grinder. These do take some practice, but some dogs handle the grinder better than clippers. Grinders leave a smoother edge on their nails that they won't scratch your skin or floors.

- Solution for Cleaning Their Ears

You need to routinely clean your puppy's ears to keep them from itching. Itching is caused by the build-up of gunk in their ears. Puppies love getting dirty, and this dirt is going to find its way into their ears.

A good cleaning solution needs to be safe and gentle for cleaning the outer part of their ear and in between the folds of the skin where bacteria love to collect. You should clean their ears once a month to reduce scratching and itchiness.

Spot cleaning with some ear wipes can help, too, especially if your pup suffers from skin problems or allergies that cause their ears to itch.

- Chew Toys

Puppies, just like human babies, are going to teethe. They are going to need things to chew. Find some tough toys that were made for chewing but are large enough that they can't swallow them. Choose quality toys in varying textures to get the puppy used to use the toys.

If you offer them rope, stuffed, or plush toys, keep in mind that your pup might ingest any of these materials. Fabric, squeakers, and stuffing could cause some digestive problems or might cause them to get choked.

During any age of their life, you need to supervise your puppy's chewing time so you can keep them from ingesting or choking on materials that aren't meant to be eaten. For a pup that is teething, do some research on the best teething toys for puppies.

Don't ever give a baby or dog a cat toy or anything that wasn't designed for puppies. These could be ingesting or choking hazards. They could also be toxic to your puppy if they were to ingest them.

- Crate or Kennel

Pick a kennel or crate that will fit your puppy well. They need to be able to turn around and stand up comfortably. Their kennel needs to be room but not so big that it makes housetraining hard to do.

If they have too much space, your puppy might be tempted to pee or poop in another part of the crate or kennel. They won't potty inside their kennel if they have to sit or lay in it.

If you just want to purchase one kennel for the life of your dog, most crates will come with divider panels so that it can grow with the puppy.

- Beds

Dog beds aren't just to make them comfortable. A good dog bed will be washable, resistant to tears, durable, and repel stains. When you are looking at a dog bed, try to find these qualities.

You might find these labeled as chew guaranteed or chew proof for puppies who are very destructive. These are more expensive but are a great investment. But this doesn't mean they aren't going to try.

Your puppy might succeed in destroying their bed. You have to realize that you won't find a bed that is totally indestructible, so if your puppy loves destroying their bed, save some money and just buy some cheap bed that you can easily replace until they grow out of this bad habit.

Beds that have removable covers are wonderful. You can take the covers off and wash them. This means you won't have to wash their bulky beds that get misshapen after they have tumbled around in a washing machine.

Large dogs might benefit from having an elevated or raised cot. This is great for warm weather climates or summer since it gets some airflow under their bed can keep your puppy cooler on hot days.

- Pet Cleaners That Are Natural

You absolutely have to have some cleaners. Your puppy is going to have some accidents. You have to be able to clean them effectively and completely, as this will lessen the chance of your puppy returning to the scene of the crime.

Try to find natural pet odor and stain removers that have active enzymes that will completely get rid of pet messes. Chemical cleaners will just cover up your pet's messes without cleaning them at all.

- Training Pads

These are great for your puppy's underdeveloped bladder. These are usually scented with some pheromones that will attract your puppy to them. These can be a great help no matter the way you will be housetraining your puppy.

Begin with putting the pads in areas that are close to where your puppy will spend their time. You could also use an exercise pen to give them some room to play while keeping them contained. This pen needs to be big enough to fit a training pad but has space for the puppy to play.

- Create a Schedule

Getting a new pet might bring up some emotions from being overwhelmingly excited to scary, and you will forget some things on your journey. The best tip I can give you when getting ready for a new puppy is to make a schedule. This doesn't have to be written in stone but will give you something to work with.

Make sure you add the steps to get your home ready, the way you will get through the first few days, what routines you will use when training, and having a schedule for activities to make sure your new puppy gets all the exercise; love, and attention it needs.

There are going to be things that you are just going to go with the flow on, and that is perfectly fine. Having a routine that your family and yourself will be able to follow will help make sure the new puppy has been transitioned into the new home as fun and seamlessly possible.

Chapter 2: Common Puppy Issues, and How to Handle Them

Do you have a new puppy that you think is absolutely adorable? Puppies are cute, and it is hard to think that in a few months, they are going to move from pleasing you to thinking "you can't stop me!" stage. This is probably a brand new world for you, and you aren't really sure what normal puppy behavior is supposed to look like. Just like normal people, puppies can develop bad habits. Yes, your puppy needs affection and love, but too much could keep them from developing good habits.

Just like when a baby cries, they might need to be changed or fed, but at other times they might want you to just hold them. This feels wonderful, but it won't help your baby become social with others and grow. Puppies are babies but just a different species. They have to learn the right way to behave so that they can grow into good dogs. They are going to test their boundaries, and this is just another part of growing, just like finding things to get into. You have the job of keeping those temptations out of their reach while realizing that they will find things to get into that you have never even thought about.

Using Play to Create Good Behaviors

The most well-intentioned owners might create behavioral problems by encouraging or reinforcing behaviors that are wrong. You might be tolerated or rewarding cute puppy behaviors that aren't going to be so cute when they are grown.

Any type of play that involves them chasing or biting might or might not cause ongoing problems as an adult dog, but playing keep-away with household items, playing catch me anytime they are called, or play biting might inadvertently create some problems. Competitive games could increase their readiness and confidence to stand up to humans. For most dogs, this won't cause problems, but there are some dogs that it isn't going to help matters. You can prevent some of these problems by being in total control over the situation. You need to teach your dog to stop running or pulling when you tell them to. When your dog stops their behavior or gives you the toy, you can throw the toy, and the game can continue. Playing with your dog is important, but you have to call the shots.

Stop Problem Behaviors Before They Begin

Other than playing keep away and stealing, normal puppy problems include getting car sick, eating poop, chewing, nipping, hyperactivity, and housetraining.

Not getting housetrained usually comes from the puppy getting too much independence too fast. You have to get back to basics, such as restricting their access to all parts of the house or crate training if you aren't home. Most puppies will pee a little when they see their owners. This is known as "submissive urination" this isn't a housetraining problem but more of the puppy not having a lot of confidence. Many puppies will grow out of this, but you can help by not exciting or intimidating your puppy or just be sure you are outside when this happens.

Being hyperactive is normally just another part of being a puppy. Certain breeds are going to be innately more active than others, but any puppy that is healthy is going to be active. Make sure your puppy gets his energy out a few times each day but NEVER force them to exercise just because you think this is going to make them tired, so they sleep longer. This could be very bad for their developing joints. The best way to make your puppy tired is by teaching him some tricks or obedience exercises or enroll him in obedience classes.

Most problem behaviors in dogs are usually mishandled or misunderstood by their owners. You might be a new dog owner, thinking about getting a dog, or just want to help your dog with some problems. Understanding the most common problems can help you solve and even prevent them. Having a solid foundation built on obedience training can help you control or prevent these problems. Let's look at some of these bad behaviors and stop them before they get started.

- Barking

Dogs are going to vocalize in some way. They might whine, howl, bark, and a lot more. Too much barking is a problem behavior. Before you can think about correcting their barking, figure out why they are being vocal. The most common barks are:

1. Responding to another dog
2. They are bored
3. They are anxious
4. They want attention
5. They feel excited
6. They are playful
7. Alerting you about something
8. Warning you about something

You need to learn how to control their excessive barking. Think about teaching them quiet and bark commands. You are going to need to be patient and consistent. Work on any underlying causes for their barking. Paying attention and being dedicated could do wonders for stopping your dog from barking.

- Biting

Puppies are going to explore their world by putting stuff in their mouth just like human babies. You might think this is cute at first, but as their teeth get bigger, this isn't going to be sweet anymore. How do you stop a puppy from biting? You have to teach them that our skin is very sensitive. They aren't trying to intentionally hurt you; they are only playing.

Just like when they play with other dogs at the park, they are going to nip at one another. Every once in a while, a puppy is going to bite a bit too hard, and the victim is going to yell in pain. The playing will stop, and the puppy will realize that they bit too hard. It won't be long before they are playing again. This is the way they learn how to bit more gently. They will make sure nobody gets hurt, and they are learning how to be gentle. You can use this method to teach them not to bite humans, too.

You can play with your puppy, and you can allow them to place your fingers into their mouth, but when they bite too hard, you need to give a bit of a yelp just like you are in pain. Allow your hand to be limp. This should startle them and make them stop biting. Once he quits biting you, they might begin licking your hand to help make you feel better. Make sure you praise them and then get back to playing. If they bite you again, repeat the process. When you yelp and startle your puppy, ignore them for about 20 seconds. If they bite you again, move away from them for about 20 seconds. If this happens three times in 15 minutes, you need to stop playing with them. If this doesn't work, you can put them in their crate for a time-out.

Once their time out is over, you can encourage them to play again. This tells them that being gentle is acceptable, and you will continue to play with them, but if playtime is painful, it is unacceptable, and you will stop playing with them. When they get to a place where they stop biting, you can begin making rules that are stricter, and you will only tolerate gentle bites. Anytime they bit you a bit too hard, give a yelp. Do the rest of the steps and slowly lessen the force of the bit you will allow.

- Chewing

This is a natural action for any age of the dog. Chewing is very important for dogs. It is just the way they have been wired. Too much chewing could turn into a problem if they destroy things. The main reason a dog begins chewing might include:

1. Curiosity
2. Anxiety
3. Too much energy
4. Bored
5. Teething

You need to encourage your dog to chew on the appropriate things by giving them lots of chew toys that don't look like household items. Try your best to keep all your personal belongings out of reach of your puppy. Anytime you aren't home, put your puppy in their crate or put them in an area where they can't destroy anything.

If you do catch your dog chewing on the wrong items, you can quickly distract them with a loud noise. You will then replace this item with one of their chew toys. The most important thing you can do is make sure your dog gets lots of exercises so they can use up their spent up energy. This will stimulate them in other ways instead of them turning to chew on things. If your puppy is teething, put an old wet washcloth into the freezer and freeze it. When they begin chewing on something they aren't supposed to, give them the frozen washcloth. The coldness will soothe their gums. Make sure you stay with them when they are chewing on the cloth, so they don't swallow any of it. You could spray deterrents on furniture or other things to keep your puppy from chewing on them. Dogs of any age need to be mentally and physically stimulated, or they are going to get bored. Boredom can lead to chewing. If your dog gets something that it shouldn't have, never chase them. They are going to view this as a game. Exchange the item they don't need for a treat.

- Digging

Dogs are going to dig. It is an instinct for them. Specific breeds such as terriers will dig more due to their hunting history. Most dogs will dig for specific reasons like:

1. To get to a new area
2. To hide their possessions
3. Trying to get comfortable
4. A hunting instinct
5. Fear
6. Anxiety
7. Too much energy
8. They are bored

Yes, it gets frustrating when your puppy digs up your yard. Try to figure out why they are digging, and then try to get rid of the source. Exercise them more, spend more time together, and work on training. If it seems inevitable that they are going to dig no matter what you do, pick out an area of your yard where they get to dig as much as they want to. Train them that this area is the only part of the yard they can dig.

- Jumping

It is a wonderful feeling when you get home from a hard day, and your puppy sees you, and they jump all over you. We look at this as them telling us, "I love you, I miss you, and here's a hug for you." This could grow into a rather dangerous habit. Even though the puppy jumping on you is endearing and cute, a dog that weighs 100 pounds might be dangerous and a bit overwhelming.

Dogs love smelling things, and to do this, they might have to jump. There are two areas where humans give off our biggest smells: the mouth and genital areas. We have all been in an uncomfortable situation where no matter what we do, we can't get a dog to move away from a specific region. If a puppy wants to reach either one of these areas, they are going to have to jump. It is hard to turn them away, and we will sometimes pick them up to calm them down. This is not a good idea. They have to learn ways to calm themselves down with their paws firmly on the ground.

This won't be easy, but with some time and persistence, you can stop this. When it is time to greet your putty, ignore him for a few minutes. This means you can't look at, talk to, or touch them. They are anxious, and they have to know once they calm down, they will get all the attention they want. NEVER give them any affection if they are jumping. They will need to calm down or sit down until you are ready to show them some affection. After they sit, you can show them some affection. This is going to be hard because you have missed them just as much as they have missed you. It is going to be worth it in the long run.

- Separation Anxiety

This is probably the most talked-about behavior problem in dogs. Ways this manifests might be defecation, urination, chewing, vocalization, or other types of destruction that happen when they are separated from us. These actions aren't necessarily the result of separation anxiety. Here are some signs of true separation anxiety:

1. They touch you anytime they can
2. They want to follow you around all the time
3. Their misbehavior happens within the first 45 minutes after you leave
4. They get anxious anytime you try to leave

Real separation anxiety is going to take some desensitization exercises, behavior modification, and dedicated training. In some very extreme cases, medications might have to be given to your dog.

- Potty Training

This is probably any pet parent's first priority. Nobody wants to come into a room and step in something that should never be on the floor. Since this is such an in-depth topic, there is a whole chapter dedicated to this subject.

- Whining

Why is my puppy constantly whining? If your puppy occasionally whines, then they might have a good reason for whining. Do they need to go pee or poop? Are they hungry? Have you given them walks? Do they need water? Can they reach their toys under the couch?

All of these are acceptable reasons for a puppy to be whining. There might be times when it becomes too much. If they are excessively whining, they have learned that whining will get them what they want. This is where whining has become a bad habit.

The first thing you need to do is make sure they are getting enough play time, exercise, and food. They might not think they are getting the right amount of these things. If their vet says that they are getting the right amounts of these things, then the puppy is fine. Try your best to stop giving them attention when they whine. Yes, it can be frustrating, but you only need to give them attention when they are quiet. Anytime you give into their whining, this is when they take total control.

You might not be meaning to, but you are actually telling them that it is fine to whine and it is a good way to communicate with you. You need to ask your dog to stop whining in a gentle tone. If they continue, repeat it louder and in an aggressive voice. This might take a few times, but it will eventually help.

- Aggression

This can be seen by biting, lunging, showing their teeth, snarling, and growling. You need to know any dog has the potential to be aggressive, and it doesn't matter their history or breed. Dogs that have abusive or violent histories and the breeds that have aggressive tendencies will exhibit more aggressive behaviors toward other dogs and people.

Some breeds have been labeled as dangerous and have been banned in specific areas. It isn't normally about the breed as much as it is about their history. Their environment can have a huge impact on their behavior, too. Many experts have agreed that breed-specific legislation will never be the answer.

The reason a dog is aggressive is the same reason why they snap and bite, but aggression is a bigger problem. If your dog does have some aggressive tendencies, talk to their vet first at it might be nothing but a health problem. If the vet doesn't find a problem or it doesn't help their aggressiveness, find an experienced dog behaviorist or trainer. You need to take some serious measures to keep people safe from your aggressive dog.

- Chasing

Dogs have an innate ability to chase anything that moves. This is all part of their predatory instincts. Most dogs will chase cars, people, and other animals. Any of these could cause devastating or dangerous outcomes. Even though you might not be able to stop your dog from wanting to chase things, you can take some steps to keep disaster away.

1. Be aware of your surroundings and look for triggers like small animals, joggers, or bicyclers.
2. Have a noisemaker or whistle to get their attention
3. Train them to come to you when you call
4. Keep them on a leash at all times

The best chance of succeeding in keeping their chasing from getting out of control is to constantly train them during their life to help them focus their attention on you.

- Begging

This is a very bad habit, but there are several dog owners who encourage it. This might lead to obesity and digestive problems. Dogs beg due to the fact they just love food. Keep in mind that table scraps are not a substitute for treats. Food also shouldn't be a substitute for your love. It is very hard to resist those looks, but if you give in just once, you are creating a big problem. You are teaching your dog that begging is allowed, and this is the wrong message to give a dog.

Before you get ready to eat, either command your dog to get in their crate, or you put them there. The crate needs to be somewhere they can't stare at you. If they behave well while you are eating, give them a special treat once you have finished eating.

- Peeing and Pooping Where They Shouldn't

This is probably the most frustrating part of being a pet parent. This could damage parts of your home and makes your dog unwelcome in public or in other people's homes. You need to talk about this behavior with their vet first to see if they have any health problems. If they don't find any medical problems, try your best to figure out if their behavior might be coming from one of these:

1. Not enough housetraining
2. Anxiety
3. Territorial marking
4. Excitement urination
5. Submissive urination

This can't be avoided in puppies, especially if they are less than one year old. Adult dogs are a different story. Some dogs might need some serious behavior modifications to get rid of this habit if it becomes ingrained.

Chapter 3: Teaching Commands

Whether you are a first-time dog owner or not, understanding the best way to train your pooch can be quite confusing. Whether you are getting a new puppy or you have adopted an adult from a shelter, we are going to go over some of the best commands to teach your dog. Whenever you, the treats, and the dog is ready, you can try out these ten commands.

What Incentives Do I Need?

Before you start teaching your dog commands, you are going to need a reward system. This is no different than any other training method. When you have a reward system, it adds a sense of accomplishment, is enticing, and establishes trust between the two of you.

First off, you are going to have to get your dog's attention. What you can use to grab their attention is going to depend on your dog. Some of them like getting food, some are happy with a toy, and others simply want affection and attention from their owner. It is also helpful if you have your dog on a leash so that you will have control over them and guide them should you need to.

When it comes to figuring out what you want to train your dog to do and what that is going to accomplish, it helps to think about where you will be training. It is a good idea to start their training in an area that is distraction-free and quiet. If you plan on using clicker training, you will need a clicker and have a pouch or pocket full of treats or toys. You also need to know what verbal cue word you are going to use, as well as a hand signal for each command.

Patience is another extremely important part of this. All training is going to take some time, and not every dog will learn in the same amount of time. Training requires perseverance and repetition.

Should They Master One Before Moving Onto Another Command?

Training isn't always easy. It can help when you add in new commands as you work, progressively introducing several at a time and then going back to them to work on them. A lot of people think that you can only teach them one command at a time, but it's okay to work on several at one time. It can add in variety and will keep your training sessions more interesting. It may also speed up the process.

Some professional dog trainers say that to teach a dog a certain command, they need to learn a basic version first. For example, if you want them to learn to shake, they are going to first have to learn how to sit. When the dog does the trick ten-time successfully, then they have learned it. When they do it 100 times successfully, then they have mastered the trick.

However, you also have to pay attention to your dog. How fast they can pick up on new things, how much they enjoy their training process, and what their personality type is all factor into the training process.

There is no dog that can completely "master" a behavior. That said, it is best to focus on a certain behavior during each training session, but ensuring that you are flexible during your training session is the most important.

Should Things be Taught in a Certain Order?

Depending on how fast your dog can pick up on new things, chances are there are a couple of different approaches that could work. Typically, it is best to start out with important life skills, such as come and sit.

When you start with the basics, it will help your dog to gain confidence in their abilities to accomplish what you would like them to do, and it will help with their overall obedience. Also, it is important that you know which commands come in handy rather than those that are "cute."

While the exact order in which your different command doesn't really matter, there is an important order to teaching your practical dog commands. This is why most people will teach their dog "come" as the first trick since it helps with their safety. You need to ensure that if your dog starts to move away from you towards something that could be threatening, you can call them back.

You should also familiarize them with their name, your voice, general training practices, and safety commands. Ensuring that they know what their name comes in handy when you need to get their attention.

When Does Training Need to Start?

Understanding the best time to start training your dog can be a bit confusing. It is a good idea to start working on training as soon as you get your new puppy. Puppies eight weeks old can be taught basic commands like stay and sit. The more advanced commands can be taught once they are six months. If you are adopting an adult dog, it's a good idea to let them adjust to their new home before you start teaching commands. This could be anywhere from a few weeks to a few months.

However, if you find that your dog is connected to you and comfortable with their new home right away, you can go ahead and start training them. This is going to help them feel like they belong, and it will establish you as their owner. When you bring a new pet into your home, there are few actions that can help to create a bond and trust with your dog that can boost your ability to train.

Should Rewards be Given Each Time?

For example, should you be giving them a treat each time they shake and sit, or should you hold the treat back to encourage them to follow commands even when an incentive isn't present? Whether or not your dog continues to get treats each time they do a command is ultimately going to be up to you and what works best for your dog.

When it comes to using positive reinforcement training, the reinforcement schedule is an important part. You need to know the frequency at which you will give them a reward. Basically, when you first start out training them, teaching them a new trick, you are going to want to reward them quickly, and each time they do the action. After they can do it consistently, you will change this up and give them a reward less often. Most of the time, you will give them a treat half the time until you can move down to only occasional rewards.

As they get better at the following command, you can reduce how many rewards they get. Treats are a very effective way to teach your dog new tricks, but you just want to make sure that you aren't rewarding them for everything little thing they do.

With that in mind, let's go over how to teach ten basic commands to your puppy. The order they show up here does not dictate the order in which you should teach them.

Come

One of the most important commands to teach your dog is how to come when they are called. Teaching them this recall command can be challenging because dogs can easily get distracted by the world around them. Every time we ask our dogs to come, we are essentially asking them to stop everything that they are doing. That means they are going to have to ignore some interesting sights, smells, foods, and dogs to return to us. This means that to build a reliable recall, we need to let our dogs know that being near us is the most fun that they could have, not to mention, it will bring the most reward.

When it comes to teaching this command, you need to make this a training game so that your dog thinks that coming to your and being around you is one of the most fantastic things ever. It's important to start this in a low-distraction area, like in your house. First, try showing them a treat or a toy, praise them for coming up to you, and then give them the reward. After a few times of this, whenever your dog looks at you and begins to move towards you, say your verbal cue. Ensure that you only use this cue when you know that your dog is coming to you.

As they get used to this, you can up the ante by asking them to come before you show them the reward. Ensure that you have a high-value you treat ready for them when they do get to you. You should also slowly start to add distance between you and your dog as you teach them the command.

You can also use some recall games to teach them the command. While you are walking your dog on the leash, get their attention, and then turn around and start to run a bit. As they start to move with you, say the verbal cue word. Then you should stop and give them their reward. You want to ensure you have their attention before you start to run so that you don't yank them with the leash.

When it comes to using the recall command, you should only have to say it once. If you have to say it multiple times, then the environment that they are in could be too distracting. It also could mean that they don't understand the common well enough.

You need to make sure that you never punish them for coming to you. You need them to associate being with you with happiness and fun. At first, you may use up a lot of treats, but it is the best way for them to learn the com command. Also, if you need to recall in an emergency situation, don't chase after them. They are going to associate this with a game and will move farther away from you.

Stay

Asking a dog to be still is a huge challenge, especially for those energized pups. To help your dog learn how to stay, you will want to start out small and make it very easy for them to do correctly. For those energetic puppies, this could mean that they only stay still for half a second. That's fine because you can build up from there.

Start teaching them in a spot that is familiar to them that is free from any tempting distractions. Ensure that your dog is focused on you by standing in front of them. Give them your full attention, and keep eye contact. Have a treat in hand, and then ask your dog to sit.

If they stay in that position for a couple of seconds, praise them and give them the treat. Continue to do this, but each time have them hold the position a bit longer before you let them have the treat.

Once they get the hang of this, you then should add in the verbal cur "stay." Once they are in a seated position, say "stay," and hold your hand out with the palm facing them. If they stay there for a couple of seconds, praise them and give them their treat. Again, continue to this, adding on another second or so.

If they are struggling to stay for the entire time, you want them to, as soon as they move, say, "Sit. Stay." Then make them stay in that position for a little less time until they get used to it. However, if you have been working on this command for a while and they typically get it right, you can repeat the verbal cue with a sharp tone, like a reprimand, if they move out of position. But you shouldn't punish them because they punish likely won't match up with the broken stay, and they will associate it with the wrong thing.

After they have learned the basic command, you can start to challenge them by walking away from them while your back is turned, when somebody is close by, or when you are trying to distract them in some way.

Touch

Touch is a name that has been given to behaviors known as hand targeting. Hand targeting is the act of a dog voluntarily touching its nose to your hand. When you teach them this, you are simply making your dog's nose a magnet. They will be drawn to the palm of your hand when it is outstretched. What makes this action useful? Hand targeting can:

- Provide your overexcited dog with a different behavior to jumping.
- Provide a reactive dog an alternative to lunging or barking.
- It helps to burn energy and makes walks less boring.
- Gives a fearful dog a safe option for meeting an unfamiliar person.
- It helps to clarify what you want from your dog.
- It can serve as a mini-recall.

Let's learn how to teach your dog to "touch." Begin by reaching your palm out to within a few inches of their nose. Your dog is going to be naturally curious about your hand and should nudge your palm. When you feel them do this, mark that by saying "yes" or using a clicker, and then give them a reward using your other hand.

Do this a total of five times.

Now, you can do this and add in your verbal cue. Say the cue word, and then place your palm out. Once they nudge your hand, repeat the rewarding process.

Do this five times.

Next, you will want to start moving your hand a bit farther away so that they will have to move forwards to nudge your hand. Again, say the verbal cue, reach your hand out, and then reward them.

Do this five times.

At this point, you can start to move even farther away from them, left your hand up so that they have to jump, or other little challenges.

Spin

Twirl doesn't serve a safety purpose, but it is a cute trick to teach your dog. To start out, you will want to begin with a basic spin. If they don't know how to stand on command, you will probably want to teach them that first.

With treats and clicker, if using one in hand, you can start teaching them how to spin. Take one of the treats and hold it close to your dog's nose and then slowly start to move the treat to the side of your dog's head. This will make them want to turn their head to follow the treat.

Continue to do this in a circle movement, all the way around their body. They should make an entire circle. After they have finished this circle, tell them "good" or "yes," or you can click the clicker. Then give them the treat.

Repeat this process several times. Once they seem to have a decent understanding of this action, add in the verbal cue "spin" before you repeat the previous steps. If you spend about five minutes each day with your dog working on the spin, they will be spinning on their own in no time.

If you want them to discern between left and right, you will do the same things we just went over, but this time you will say "right spin" or "left spin" depending on which direction you are moving them in.

Leave It

Dogs like to grab up things that they shouldn't, and you need to know that they will drop it when you tell them to. When it comes to teaching them the leave it command, you are really teaching them to ask for permission. You won't always see something they shouldn't have before they have time to grab it up, so you want them to look to you to get permission before they pick something up off the ground.

You can teach this through free-choice exercises. To do this, place a treat in your fist. Allow your dog to try and get the treat out of your hand any way they want, including nosing, pawing, and licking your hand.

Once they stop trying to take the treat from you, mark this with a click or by saying "yes." You will immediately open your hand and tell them, "take it," and give them the treat. By doing this, you are showing them that you don't want them to pay attention to the treat.

After doing this a few times, your dog should start to step away from your fist or simply ignore the treat. Then you can wait a couple of seconds longer before you tell them to "take it."

Then, place the treat in your open palm so that your dog sees it at all times. If they try to take the treat, close your fist, and wait a bit until they ignore it. Once their attention has turned away from the treat, you can tell them to "take it."

Once you have that "take it" command down, you can start to leave things on the floor.

Lay the treat on the floor and let your hand rest over it. Once again, let them try to take the treat out from under your hand. Once they stop trying, mark this and give them the reward. However, don't give them the treat that you place on the floor. While you could do like before and give them the treat with the "take it" cue, you want them to learn that this is not about eventually getting an item. After all, if you dropped medication on the floor, it is never going to be up for grabs. Instead, give them a treat from out of your pocket or your other hand. It is best if the reward is a higher value than what you placed on the floor.

Once they easily ignore covered items on the floor, you can remove your hand. You need to be ready to cover it up if need be. You want your dog to ignore those uncovered treats, but you also want to ensure that they don't get that food at all. Once they look away, leans back, or show some sort of disinterest to the uncovered food, mark this action and give them a treat.

You can then move to place your dog on the leash and standing. This time you will be covering the treat with your foot, and the leash will serve as extra insurance that they don't get the food on the floor.

Once they have gotten good at ignoring the food, you can introduce the cue "leave it" when you drop something on the floor. Before you drop the food on the floor, say "leave it," and drop the food. Eventually, you won't have to use the cue, but it does come in handy sometimes.

Place/On Your Bed

To train your dog to go to their place is a great way to get them out from under your feet. It's important they know how to lie down before you try to teach them this. Before you teach this, come up with a verbal cue. You can use "place," but "mat" or "bed" also works.

Start by luring your dog to their mat or bed. Say the command and then use a treat to get them onto the spot. Once all four of their feet are on their bed, praise them and then give them the treat. Do this several times until they come to the bed on command.

Next, you will add in the "lie down" command. Once they have all four paws on the mat, have them lie down. After a while, they will understand the command "place," which means they should get on their mat and lie down, and you won't have to do both commands.

Once they are consistently lying down on their mat when you say "place," you can start to increase the amount of time they stay on their mat before they get their treat. You can then start removing yourself from the room and seeing if they stay on their mat. Another choice is to see if they will go to their mat no matter what room you have it placed in.

Back

This command will get your dog to back up. To teach this, have your dog standing in front of you. Starting this out in a hallway is a good choice as it keeps them focused. Facing each other, take a step towards them, and once they back up, mark this with a "yes" or click, and give them a treat. Continue to do this until they have the movement down, and then you can start adding in the "back" command. Eventually, you can just say "back," and they will move backward on their own without you moving.

Once they have learned this, you can start having them back up even when you are standing in front of them.

Sit

One of the first commands everybody teaches their dog to do is to sit. After all, when they are sitting, they won't be jumping on you. However, getting them to sit for more than a few seconds can be difficult because they like to pop back up.

With a pocket full of treats, start with your dog standing. Take a treat and hold it to their nose. Slowly lift the treat over their head towards the backside. As they lift their head to follow the treat, their bottom should dropdown.
Once they have come to a seated position, praise or click the clicker, and then give them the treat. Get them back into a standing position and then repeat the previous steps.

Once they start to follow the treat into the seated position, you can get rid of the lure. Ensure your lure hand is empty, have them sit, and then give them a treat from your other hand. The movement you make with the empty had is the hand signal for the movement. You can then start adding in the verbal cue of "sit" before you give them the hand signal. Eventually, they won't need the hand signal.

Pushing your dog's hind end down can be confusing and intimidating, so don't use that method.

Lay Down

Once they know how to sit, you can teach your dog how to lie down. Get your dog to sit, and with the treat in hand, hold it close to their nose and then move it towards the chest and then to the floor.

They should be following this motion down into a lying position. When they are lying down, mark this with praise and a treat. Do this until they can easily follow the treat into the down position. At that point, you can start to add in the word "down."

As long as your dog is lying down, give them treats. This will help to increase the amount of time they spend lying down.

Shake

The last command is the classic handshake. You don't have to physically pick up your dog's paw to teach him this command.

Start by holding your hand out to your dog. Expect your dog to experiment to figure out what you want, like licking or sniffing. The key here is to just way and not say a word. Once your dog paws at your hand, praise or click, open your hand and then give them a treat.

Do this several times until they start to consistently paw your hand when you put it in front of them.
Once they are doing this consistently, start to build up the time and increase the difficulty. Have them keep their paw on your hand for a bit longer than before, and then praise and give them a treat. You aren't giving them any verbal cues yet.

Get them to a point where they let their paw rest on your hand for a while before you praise and give them a treat. You want them to understand it's not the pawing at your hand that is being rewarded.

Once they consistently hold their paw in your hand for a few seconds, add in the command shake. Eventually, you move up to an open palm, and the word "shake," and they should instinctively place their paw into your hand.

Chapter 4: Seven Simple Steps to Housebreaking

When you get a new puppy, the most important thing you need to do is get your puppy housebroken. Nobody wants to find a mess on their floor. Potty training a puppy seems straightforward because, in theory, you just need to teach them when and where to pee or poop. But in reality, it can be a lot more challenging than what you think.

The good news is that there are some techniques and tricks that will help make this process easier for you so you can see success. Keep reading to find out how to potty train your puppy.

You need to begin potty training as quickly as you possibly can. It doesn't matter if you rescued an adult dog from a shelter or an eight-week-old from a breeder. Yes, adult dogs might have to be housebroken, too. You can successfully potty train a dog of any age by using these techniques and tips. Adult dogs might learn a lot quicker because they have more control of their bladder.

- Create a Schedule and Stick With It

In order to stay away from accidents, you need to take your puppy outside so they can potty fairly frequently. How often is it frequently? Since you are just starting their potty training, you need to take them out first thing each morning. Try your best to do this at the same time every day. From that point, you need to take them out once an hour and especially right before putting them to bed. Remember that there are some dogs that might have to go more.

It would be a good idea to take your puppy outside before and after:

1. Exciting events

2. Drinking
3. Eating
4. Playing
5. Sleeping

This list might seem like a lot of bathroom breaks. As your puppy gets bigger, so does their bladder control. If you see your puppy scratching at the door, whining, sniffing the floor, or circling in a particular spot, these are all common signs that they need to go potty. By the time they are six months, they might be able to go about six hours without needing to go potty. They really should get to go potty more frequently than this.

Other than scheduling their potty time, you need to feed them at the same time every day. You could limit their access to water a few hours before their bedtime if you don't want to have to get up and let them out in the middle of the night or clean up their mess.
Everything that goes in has to come out. Mealtimes will influence your puppy's need to go potty.

- Create An Outside Potty Zone

If you want to keep your puppy from pottying in places they shouldn't, you have to make it clear where they should go by creating a potty area in the corner of your yard.

By the time your puppy is eight weeks old, they will decide where they like to go potty. This place might be potty pads, a specific spot of carpet, dirt, mulch, linoleum in the laundry room, concrete patio, or grass.

This basically means that they probably have an idea about where they want to go. You are going to have to communicate to them where YOU want them to go. Each time you take them out to the potty, direct them to the potty zone. With some time, they are going to learn to associate this spot with going to the bathroom.

What about potty pads? If you can't take your puppy outside as frequently as possible, you could put down some potty pads or newspaper. You have to understand that this could slow down your puppy's progress or condition them to only use these materials.

- Use The Same Command

If you don't give your command to go potty, their potty breaks might take some time. There are a lot of things to inspect and smell when they are outside. The easiest solution would be to help them associate a specific phrase or word with going to the bathroom. I have always used the phrase "go potty" for animals and my own daughter. Whatever you decide to use, you need to say it when:

1. Your puppy starts doing its business
2. You direct your puppy to their potty place
3. You take your puppy outside

Contrary to what many people think, dogs are very smart. It won't be long before your puppy learns that "go potty" means it is time to go outside and either pee, poop, or both.

Can you housetrain your puppy using a bell? Training your puppy to let you know when they need to go potty is a good way to stay away from accidents. The easiest way to accomplish this is by hanging a bell on the doorknob of the door you go out when you take your puppy outside to the potty. When you walk out that door, ring the bell. Only ring the bell when you are taking them out to the potty. Don't ring it for anything else, or they could associate the bell with just going outside.

It won't be long before they pick up on this, and they might try to ring the bell when they feel the need to go potty. If they do this, immediately give them some praise and take them outside. This reinforces the behavior you want from them.

- Celebrate The Good Times

The most critical step when house training your pup is making them feel wonderful about going to the potty where they are supposed to go. Most dogs want to please their humans, and this can be used to your advantage.

Once they have finished going potty, and I mean right, when they do their business, give them praise, love, and treats. They will soon learn that going to the potty where they are supposed to be going to be in their best interest.

What are they won't potty? If your dog doesn't do their business within a couple of minutes after you take them outside, just take them back in and try again in about 30 minutes. Just stay alert and look for any sign that they might have to go.

- Confine or Supervise

If you want your puppy to be successful at potty training, you have to watch them for any sign that they may need to potty. To make this easier on you, you need to keep them close to you at all times.

What if you aren't around your puppy all the time? How can you house train your puppy if you have to run an errand or go to work?

The best thing would be for somebody like a relative, pet sitter, friend, or neighbor to take them outside for you. If this isn't possible, try to put them in their crate or other space where they have enough room to turn around, lie down, and stand up when you aren't home.

This is known as crate training. Dogs will naturally stay away from going potty where they sleep or eat; this will encourage them to hold it in until they can get outside.

How often should puppies go potty? Many puppies will be able to control their bladders for at least one hour for each month of age and plus one. This means that a puppy that is three months old should handle going about four hours without having an accident. They might go longer if they aren't active or sleeping like overnight.

Use this rule of thumb to figure out if you should go home on your lunch break or find somebody to help you out when you are away. Keep in mind, each dog is going to be different, and the smaller the dog, the smaller the bladder, so they won't be able to wait as long. Find what is best for your puppy.

- Handle Any Accident the Right Way

If you ask me, all puppies are perfect. But accidents are going to happen. If they do happen, take a few deep breaths and do this:

1. Interrupt their pottying by making a loud noise like clapping your hands
2. Immediately take them outside
3. Give them a reward if they finish peeing outside

Be sure you clean up their mess well when you get back inside. Try your best to find an enzyme cleaner that will get rid of any odors to reduce the risk of having more accidents. Once you have cleaned up, take their excrement or used paper towels outside to their potty place.

Yes, this is a bit gross, but it will reinforce to your puppy where they need to go potty. NEVER punish the puppy if they do make a mistake. They aren't going to make the right connection. Rubbing their nose or scolding them only scares or confuses them.

The only way to handle this situation is to redirect them and celebrate when they go.

- Hang in There

If you follow the steps in this chapter, you are on the fast track to your puppy's success, and you should have them potty trained in no time. It is important for you to keep in mind that your puppy is only a baby who has a lot to learn.

You might be wondering how long it will take to potty train your puppy. It might take you a few days, or it might take you almost a year to completely get your puppy potty trained. It basically is all up to how you train, how quickly you begin, the puppy's history, and their previous habits.

With that being said, if you think that things are taking a lot longer than they should be, talk to your vet to be sure your puppy doesn't have any health problems like bladder infections that might be keeping them from progressing.

Chapter 5: Crate Training

Having a well-behaved dog is something that we all want, and crate training is a big part of that. It gives them a safe environment that also teaches them independence and responsibility. While many see crates as "caging up" a dog, they are naturally denning animals, and they like to be in enclosed spaces. It makes them feel calm and secure.

The main purpose of crate training your dog is housetraining since dogs aren't a fan of soiling their dens. Te crate will limit their access to your house while they are learning the rules that they have to follow, such as not chewing up the furniture. Crates will also give you a safe way to transport your dog.

Before we get into learning how to crate train, let's go over some important rules. If you don't use crate training correctly, the dog could feel frustrated and trapped.

1. You should never use their crate as a punishment. Your dog will start associating their crate with fear and will refuse to use it.
2. Don't make your dog stay in its crate for too long. A dog that gets crated all night and day won't get the exercise they need or the human interaction they should have, which can make them anxious or depressed. You might have to change up your schedule, get a pet sitter, or take them to dog daycare to reduce the time they are in their crate.
3. Puppies who are under six months old shouldn't be in the crate for longer than three or four hours. They are unable to control the bowels or bladder for longer than that. The same is true for adult dogs who are just being housetrained.
4. Crate the dog until they can be trusted to be alone in the house without being destructive or having any accidents. At that point, you can graduate them to an

enclosed area of the house, such as the kitchen, before you let them have full home access while you're away. The crate needs to have a comfy bed and be open so that the dog can go inside whenever they feel like it.

Picking the Right Crate

The first thing you need to do is to pick out the right crate. It should be flexible, durable, and comfortable. If your dog likes to sleep in the dark, you could go with airline or kennel crates because they are fully enclosed, while other dogs may prefer a wire crate. You also don't want to get a crate that is too big for your dog.

When it comes to size, you want to ensure that the crate is just big enough where they have the ability to comfortably stand up and turn inside. If your dog is a puppy and still has growing to do, pick a crate size that is going to accommodate the size they will be as an adult. In this case, you will want to block off the excess crate space so that they don't go to the other end to use the bathroom. Animal shelters will sometimes rent ours creates. By renting, you can trade-in for a bigger size as your puppy grows, and so they are an adult, you can buy a permanent crate.

Once you have the crate, add stuff to it to make your puppy comfortable. Towels or dog beds should be used so that they have something nice to lay one. You will need to also take cues from your dog. If they start tearing the dog bed apart, or they pee on it, then you will have to try something different. If it turns out that they prefer to just sleep on the cage without any padding, that's okay too. Sometimes dogs prefer a hard surface.

The Training Process

The process of crate training can take days or weeks, depending on how old they are, their past experiences, and their temperament. There are two things that you need to keep in mind while you are crate training. First, the crate needs to be associated with something pleasant. Second, training should be done over the course of several small steps. You don't want to try to take things too quickly.

1. Introduce them to their new crate.

Set the crate up in a place in your house where you and your family tend to spend plenty of time. For most people, this would be the living room or the family room. Lay a towel or blanket in the crate and remove the door. Allow them to explore the crate on their own. Some dogs are naturally curious and will begin sleeping in their new home right away. If your dog is not one of those:

- Take them to the crate and talk to them in a happy voice. Ensure that the door is open and secured so that it doesn't end up hitting your dog and scaring them.
- Encourage them to go into the crate by placing some treats nearby, just in the door, and one all the way inside of the crate. If they still refuse to go inside, that's fine. Don't force them to go into the crate.
- Continue to toss them treats in the crate until they calmly go inside to give them food. If they aren't interested in treats, try using their favorite toy.

This step of the process could go by quickly, or it could end up taking several days. Like I said before, don't rush this. You want them to associate the crate with happy things, not scary things.

2. Give your dog a meal inside of their crate.

Once you have introduced your dog to their create, start to feed them their meals near their create. This is going to help them create pleasant associations to the crate.

- If they have been going into their crate easily at this point, but their food dish all the way at the back.
- If they are still reluctant to go inside, place the dish only to the point in which they are willing to go inside without them feeling anxious. Every time you fee them there, place the dish just a bit further back.
- After they have started to stand comfortably in the crate to eat, you can start to close their door as they eat. The first time, ensure you open the door back up as soon as they are done eating. With every other feeding, leave the door close a bit longer until they stay inside for ten minutes or so after they have eaten.
- If they start to whine about being let out, you could have upped the amount of time they spend inside too fast. Next time, shorten the amount of time they stay in there. If they start to cry or whine, you should keep the door shut and not open it immediately. Otherwise, they will associate whining with being let out, and they will continue to whine.

Again, this step can take several days or weeks.

3. Practice making them stay in the crate longer.

Once your dog is regularly eating their meals in the crate without showing signs of anxiety or fear, you can put them in there for short periods of time while you are at home.

- Call them to their crate and give them a treat.
- Present them with a command, like "crate," and then encourage them by pointing into the crate with a treat held in your hand.
- After they get into the crate, praise them, let them have a treat, and then close the door.
- Quietly sit near the crate for five to ten minutes and then head to a different room of the house for a few minutes. Come back and sit quietly for a little while and then let them out.

- Continue to do this over the next few days and gradually increase the amount of time you let them stay in the crate and the amount of time you stay out of sight.
- After your dog starts there, quietly, for 30 minutes with you mainly out of sight, you can start to leave them crated whenever you leave the house for short periods or letting them sleep there at night.

This process can end up taking several days or weeks.

4. Start crating your dog whenever you leave the house.

Once your dog stays in the crate for 30 minutes without becoming afraid or anxious, you can start to leave them in their crate for short periods of time whenever you go somewhere.

- Put them into their crate using the same commands you have been and a treat. You can also give them a couple of safe toys that they can play with within the crate.
- You can change up the moment during your "getting ready to leave" routine to place them in their crate. While you don't want them to hang out in their crate for a long time before you actually leave, you can place them in the crate five to 20 minutes before you leave.
- Don't make the departure prolonged or emotional. You want them to be matter-of-fact. Give them brief praise, a treat for going into the crate, and then leave.

When you get back home, you want to keep things low-key as well. This will keep you from increasing their anxiety over your return. You should continue to crate them for short periods while you're at home so that they don't start associating being crated for being left alone.

5. Put them in their crate at night.

You will place them in their crate with the regular command and a treat. At first, you may want to have their crate in your room or close by in the hallway, especially when they are young. Puppies tend to have to go outside and use the bathroom during the night, so it's important that you can hear them whine when they need to go. You will also want to keep older dogs close by so that they don't associate the crate with isolation.

After the dog has started to sleep well all night with the crate close to you, you can start to move it to the location you would like it to be.

To help get your puppy ready for bed, you should let them play as hard as they want. Some nighttime zoomies can help burn up some energy so that they are ready to go to sleep at bedtime. However, you may want to go with some calmer play options. Fetch, or tug-o-war can be over-stimulating for some puppies. Playing some games like sniffari is a great low-impact way to help them burn off some excess energy.

Mental exercises can also be helpful to do before bedtime. Give them some interactive toys and puzzles that they can play with to help them settle down. Enrichment activities throughout the day can also help them. Having an established bedtime routine that they are used to will go a long way in making crate training go easier.

Possible Problems

Your dog may start whining when you leave them in the crate at night. When this happens, it can be hard to figure out if they are whining about being let out or if they need to go use the bathroom. If you have followed the steps that we went over, then you have rewarded them for whining in the past by being let out of the crate. If this is how you have been doing things, then try not to pay any attention to their whining. If you believe that they are trying to test you to see if you will let them out, then they will likely stop the whining. Pounding on the crate or yelling at them is only going to make things worse.

If they continue to whine after you have ignored them for a few minutes, use the phrase they are familiar with when going outside to use the bathroom. If they respond to that, then take them out. This trip outside should be one of purpose and not play. If you are convinced that they don't need to use the bathroom, the best thing to do is to continue ignoring them until they quit whining. You should not give in. If you do, it is going to tell them that if they continue to whine loud and long enough, they are going to get what they want. If you didn't try to rush through the steps to get them to crate trained, it is less likely that you will encounter this issue. If it becomes unmanageable, you might want to start the crate training process all over again.

If you have a brand new puppy, then they may experience distress barking. This can be in the form of howls, barks, or whines and is common for puppies who are still new to the home. There is an adjustment period when you bring on a new puppy that takes some time, and it is normal for them to get stressed out in a new routine and environment. They are moving from sleeping with their littermates and mother to being by themselves can be stressful. Distress barking is characterized by non-stop, high-pitched howling or barking or long periods of whining. It could be paired with the puppy pacing around their crate, panting, trying to escape from the crate, or excessive licking.

A new puppy should receive some comfort if they are distressed barking. The main thing is to make sure you are comforting them and not coddling them. Speak to them using a soothing voice and praise them when they show a calmer behavior. If need be, you can sit next to the crate to let them know you are close by. If you can, avoid taking them out of their crate. Again, you don't want to teach them that barking will help them get out of the crate. However, it can be helpful to open the door and pet them while they are inside to help them settle down.

If your dog suffers from separation anxiety and you are looking to use crate training as a remedy, it isn't going to fix anything. While the crate can keep them from becoming destructive, it could cause them to get injured while trying to escape. You can only solve separation anxiety through desensitization and counterconditioning procedures. You may need to reach out to an animal behavior specialist.

The last thing you need to ensure is that you aren't leaving your dog in their crate for too long. Depending on their age, there is an amount of time in which your pup can "hold it." A good rule of thumb is the number of months old they are, plus one. That means for a two-month-old puppy, you should be able to expect them to wait three hours between necessary potty breaks. For a three-month-old puppy, it would be four hours. Six-month-olds should be able to wait a max of seven hours.

When it comes to overnight, you can extend this time a bit if they are sleeping. Once they are 16 weeks, most puppies can handle six to seven hours of overnight crating.

Chapter 6: Creating a Schedule

The structure is the best way to help your new puppy know what to expect during the day and to feel secure. A great way to bring this into your home is to come up with a schedule that works for everybody and then follow through with it. The first few weeks after you get your new puppy is when you should be focused on developing their good behaviors. It's also not just the puppy who will benefit from a schedule. It is going to make the lives of all of the human family members easier. Every moment of your puppy's day doesn't have to be planned out, but there are important parts of your puppy's day where the schedule can make all of the difference between complete chaos and a well-adjusted pooch.

The work you put in now in coming up with a schedule is going to pay off in the long run. Once you have a full-grown dog, they will be well-behaved. At first, it can be hard to figure out what you want the routine to look like and what will work best for you, everybody in the house, and the dog, but you need to ensure that this doesn't take too long to figure out. The following are some things you should consider when it comes to creating a schedule.

1. Feeding

Your puppy is working on becoming a big and healthy full-grown dog, but they had to eat enough food to do so, and that means they will need to be fed more often than an adult dog. While adult dogs may only get fed once or twice a day, a puppy should get three square meals. Does that sound like it is going to require a bit of work? The great thing is that all you need to do is schedule their meals around when you would normally eat your meals. The best time to feed them is at seven in the morning, noon, and five at night. This should be followed for the first three to four months of their lives.

After that, the feedings can be changed to only twice a day, unless you have been told by their vet that they are going to require more frequent meals. Creating a feeding schedule for your dog is very important. When you have a set feeding schedule, your dog is going to learn when they can expect food and is going to be less likely to beg for something between their meals.

2. Potty Time

Unless you are a fan of having to clean up messes, you will want to establish potty times for your puppy that happen every two to four hours. If you make them wait any longer, then there is a good chance that they are going to have an accident. When you place a set time and place for this, will teach them that pottying isn't something they should do whenever and wherever they want.

3. Keywords Training

While you might not be able to put your young puppy into formal training classes just yet, you can still take the time to start teaching them some basic things. Keywords are something that every puppy should be able to start learning. Start out with important like "bad," "no," and "good." These words should stay simple and be consistent. Your dog needs to get accustomed to hearing the same words so that they create a connection with the meaning every time you use them.

4. Play and Exercise

Your puppy can bring some fun and joy into your life. That's why it's important to schedule time into your day for play and exercise. Ideally, their day should start with exercise before they have their first meal. Once they have breakfast, a nice walk can be taken to strengthen your bond with them. You are going to repeat things throughout the day.

Strenuous and sustained exercises, such as jumping and long runs, aren't healthy for small puppies. Better choices are games that cause mental stimulation, some running in the yard and simple playing are all good for them. Some experts will tell you that it is best to wait until they are a year old before you let them take some serious exercise, but this could vary depending on their breed. Various breeds of dogs come with differing energy levels and growth rates. This means that the growth plates that they have within their joints close up at varying ages. You should still schedule exercise and playtimes into their day. Several short sessions are a lot better for a puppy than letting them play for a long time.

5. Bedtime and Naps

Young puppies will sleep quite a bit. In fact, some of them may sleep 16 to 18 hours. You should schedule some time into the day for nap time. Family members need to know that they should not disturb them while they are sleeping, especially the younger ones. They need to get their rest. This is where crate training can be helpful because you can put their crate in a quiet area where they won't be distracted.

As for bedtime, some owners prefer to give their dogs a set bedtime for them to settle down. Some allow them to sleep whenever they sleep. You might find, though, that it is easier on a puppy if you have a set bedtime that they get used to.

Is a Schedule Necessary?

The sooner you can come up with a schedule for them, the sooner they can adjust to their new family. Routine makes things easier for everybody, humans included, to know what they should and shouldn't do and what is expected. Remember that the cute little accidents and craziness that come out of a puppy won't be so cute once they are a full-grown dog.

When you have a routine, it can help reduce anxiety in your dog. If the dog's day is unpredictable, it can end up elevating their stress. Dogs like it when things are predictable, especially in regards to their basic needs of safety, food, and shelter. Like with every other living being, survival and safety are of the utmost importance. Routines give them a predictable stream of information about their main needs. This information is what is going to lower their stress and allows the dog to move on and enjoy their life.

Routines are also very helpful when it comes to house training your pooch. Keeping things regular is a big part of making the house training process successful. When they are first learning associations about where they should potty, routines help them remember the associations. When you stick to regular bathroom times during house training, the dog is going to be less likely to have an accident. If they are experiencing a sense of urgency in needing to going, they are going to be more likely to "hold it" if they know they are going to be taken out soon.

Having feeding routines will help keep them from gaining a lot of weight. When you leave food out for your dogs all day long, it can cause weight gain or cause them to overeat. When you establish a routine with their feeding times, it can keep you from overfeeding them. If they get used to eating a certain amount of food and certain times during the day, they are going to be less likely to beg for treats or food.

Routines also play a big part in training them. If you are trying to teach them tricks or commands, sticking to using the same types of verbal commands and hand signals will help them learn. Consistency is important to dogs, and this is especially true when it comes to training. Remember that it is very important that everybody in the house is on the same page when it comes to rain. If everybody stays consistent, it will reduce the chance of the dog getting confused and giving up.

We'll go over a sample schedule that you can use as a starting point. Your schedule should work for you and your pup. You don't have to change your entire life to make a schedule that works.

- First thing each day (7 AM to 7:30 AM) – Take them out so that they can use the bathroom. Once they have taken care of business, play and interact with them for a bit. This is also a good time to give them a once over to check and see if anything is unusual about their eyes, fur, attitude, demeanor, and more.

- Breakfast (8 AM to 9 AM) – Give the puppy their first meal of the day. Only have the food down for them to eat for 15 minutes. Once those 15 minutes are up, they up their food and don't put it down again until it is time for the next meal. You can still give them treats throughout the day when training. Give them clean water.

- After breakfast (9 AM to 10 AM) – Puppies will typically need to use the bathroom again after they have eaten, so give them another chance to go. After this, you should spend some time with them training or playing. While everybody tends to be busy getting ready for school or work, take some time to take them for a quick walk to use the potty just one more time.

- Mid-morning (10 AM to 12 PM) – Ideally, they should spend the rest of the morning napping, preferably in a pen or crate. Even if you're home during this time, they need to spend a bit of time within their pen or crate. This is going to teach them how to be alone. You also want to know what kind of trouble your puppy might get into if you aren't paying attention to them, and you need to have a place where you can put them when you can't be supervising them. If they are going to be home alone past their next potty break, you may want to have a pen set up for them in a place where they can use the bathroom. Another option is to have somebody check in on them and take them for a walk.

- Noon (12 PM to 1 PM) – This should be a repeat of their morning routine. Once they wake up, let them go outside. Feed them lunch, and then take another trip outside. You should spend some time with them playing, and don't forget to let them have another potty break before they take their next nap.

- Mid-afternoon (1 PM to 5 PM)– Once they wake up, they need to go out. They can play or train once more and then let them go use the bathroom once more. When at home during this time, let them spend some time with you before it is time for dinner.

- Dinner (5 PM to 7:30 PM) – If you have been planning their mealtimes around yours, it is going to be natural to feed them while you are cooking or while you are eating. The main thing is to ensure you are paying attention so that you can take them out once they are done eating. Before your family sits down to eat, it may help to give your puppy a chew toy that they can play with within their crate. This will keep them from being underfoot, and you won't have to worry about anybody giving them table scraps.

- Evening (7:30 PM to 11 PM)– They will need to go use the bathroom once more. This is the best time of the day for them to get more interaction from you. This tends to be the "witching hour" for most puppies, and if you are ready for this by initiating play, it could help them to settle down. If that doesn't work, even after they have had a lot of exercises, let them have a treat and ask them to get into their crate to calm down. You can take them for an evening stroll to give them another chance to use the potty and ensure that they potty right before bed.

- Bed – Their adjustment to their new home will be a lot easier when they have a set bedtime, and it also makes it easier to housebreak them. It won't matter if this time is eight PM or midnight. The important thing is to keep it regular. Have them get into their crate and then do what you normally do to get them to settle down.

- Night – If they are unable to hold themselves all night just yet, you will want to set the alarm so that you can get up and time them out to use the bathroom. It is better that you get up before they do so that you don't respond to their barking and whining. Then put them back to bed.

When you make a point of establishing some sort of routine from the get-go, you are going to have a better chance of having a more well-behaved dog. While routines and schedules are very important and helpful for dogs, it is also important that you and the dog can stay flexible so that everybody is ready for any changes that might happen.

The dog still needs to be able to function even if its routine gets broken for some reason. A dog needs to be adaptable if they are going to be able to move through their life without any unnecessary stress. To do this, you should make small adjustments to how you time the schedule or make some variations to their routine.

When it comes to setting up routines, it is important that you are realistic and establish a routine that is going to work for your life. Dogs can deal with some changes, so if you need to alter the routine to fit into your schedule, then you can do so. The dog is going to be much better off if you find a routine that you can stick with rather than constantly facing uncertainty.

Chapter 7: Reading Your Dog

The body language of a dog involves a series of unique movements that communicate intentions and emotions. Their body language tends to be very different from the body language of humans. A number of their communication methods are made up of growls, barks, and whines, so you should ensure you understand what each of those sounds means. Most of the time, dogs rely on the use of nonverbal body language. This is why there can be a lot of misunderstandings between the dog and the human. Sometimes, their body language is completely foreign to us. Then there are times that it is completely opposite to a similar signal that humans use, like looking away or yawning. To better understanding what your pooch is telling you, let's go over some dog body language you should know.

Tail Wagging

Tail wagging may seem like one of the most obvious forms of body language, but it's not. A wagging tail does not necessarily mean that your dog is happy. This is one of the most commonly misinterpreted signals of all time. The dog is experiencing some type of emotional arousal whenever they wag its tail. It might be that they are excited, or it could be they are frustrated or worse. To really know how your dog is feeling, you need to pay attention to the direction and speed at which its tail is wagging and how it is positioned

Simply put, the faster they are wagging their tail, the more excited they are. You have likely seen your dog wage their tail in long, slow, side-to-side motions when they greet you, and it often moves their entire body. This lets you know that they are relaxed. When their wage is faster and twitch-like, it shows more arousal, and it could indicate something negative. This dog is on alert about something.

The tail's direction can clue you in on some things. They could also have the helicopter tail wage where it spins in a circle. There is no doubt about that wage. It is a happy wage. You are going to see this whenever they get to see a person that they love.

Finally, how their tail is oriented with the ground can tell you a lot about how they are feeling. Essentially, if they are feeling assertive, the tail is going to be higher up. If they have the tail pointed down or tucked between their legs, they could be feeling stressed or fearful. If you notice that they are holding the tail up like a flag, they feel confident and possibly a bit aggressive. Relaxed dogs will have their tails held in their natural neutral position, but this neutral is going to depend on your dog and its breed. For example, breeds like the Chow Chow have a neutral tail position where their tail curls over their back. Then you have dogs like the Italian Greyhound, where they have a low, neutral position. Once you know what their neutral is, you will find it easier to spot what their emotions are.

Raised Hackles

Raised hackles simply mean that you will see their hair stand on end. The fancy term for this is piloerection and allows the fur along the shoulders and down the back to fluff up. This definitely lets you that something has gotten your dog's attention, but it doesn't mean that they are upset. The dog could be stressed or upset, but it could also mean that they are really interested in something or excited. This movement of their skin is normal involuntary, a lot like how we can get goosebumps.

Posture

How a dog has their weight disturbed across their paws can let you know a lot about their intention and mood. For example, pick a dog that is cowered and hunched down. This is a clear sign of stress or fear. They could be trying to remove themselves from what they are afraid of, and this posture makes them look smaller. Basically, it tells you, "I mean no harm." This could go a step further when they roll over onto their back and exposes their belly. In a relaxed dog, this is them asking for a belly rub. However, it may show you that they are feeling anxious or stressed. If that be the case, they might end up urinating a bit.

The opposite of this is if they are standing with most of their weight on their front paws. This means that they are trying to move close to something. This could mean that they are interested in something, but it could mean that they have offensive intentions, especially if you notice this happening along with aggressive cues, such as a high tail that is twitching. This could indicate that they want to make themselves look bigger.

An easy-to-understand posture cue is when they bow. This occurs whenever they drop their chest to the group and raise their butt in the air. As you could guess from the name, they do this to initiate play without people and other dogs.

One of the harder-to-understand signals is the paw raise. When you have a pointing breed, such as the English Setter, a paw raise has to do with their pointing action when they spot prey. When you aren't dealing with those types of breeds, raised paws could show that they are feeling uncertain or insecure.

Facial Expressions

The facial features of dogs are very similar to people's, but the meanings behind those expressions aren't typically the same. Let's take yawning, for example. People yawn when they are bored or tired, but a dog yawns when it feels stressed. Dogs like to yawn to calm themselves if they are feeling stressed, and they will use it to help calm other people, which includes their owner. You may even want to try yawning at your pooch when you know they are feeling stressed, like when you take them to the vet. Don't be surprised if they were to yawn back at you.

Lip-licking is often misinterpreted. Lip licking will often happen after they have eaten, just like humans do, but will also do this if they are feeling anxious. The tongue flick can be very quick and hard to notice. They aren't telling you they want to lick your face, but instead, they are feeling discomfort in a certain situation.

The smile tends to be one of the most confusing expressions. Yes, there are dogs that do smile; if you don't know this expression very well, it can look scary. They typically warn you that they aren't happy when they bare their teeth. It's like they are saying, "look at my weapons." It's very hard to mistake that time of snarl, especially when they are growling. You will see that the corners of their mouth are turned up to create a C, and you can see all of their front teeth.

When a dog is just smiling, they will show their front teeth, but you will be able to tell that the meaning behind it is completely different. What some people call the submissive grin lets you know that they are happy, especially if they are wiggly and loose. Their overall attitude is letting your know, "hello, I come in peace."

Eyes

A lot can be learned by looking at a dog's eyes. First, they could either have hard or soft eyes. Soft eyes are characterized by relaxed eyelids, and it may even appear as though they are squinting. This could mean that they are happy or calm. Hard eyes are when their eyes seem to be cold. These let you know that your dog is not all that happy, and it is going to be very clear when you look at them. It could be that they are guarding a toy, or they might feel aggressive towards somebody or something. A dog that is looking intently at something may have a hard start, especially if they are holding the look for a long time, and this could mean that they see a threat.

Their eye contact with you or something else should also be paid attention to. Much like how a hard start could mean aggression, looking away could be used to calm a situation. If they are feeling stressed, they are going to turn their gaze away from you. We often think they are ignoring us and being stubborn, but they are really showing discomfort.

The whites of their eyes can also let you in on some important information. What is called "whale eyes," the dog will show you the whites of the eyes and is letting you know that they are feeling stressed or anxious. This can be seen when you make them uncomfortable, such as patting them on the head or if they are afraid that somebody is going to take their toy or bone.

With all of that in mind, let's look at some combinations of body language cues and what they mean.

1. Relaxed approachable

Relaxed and approachable dogs will have their ears up but not forward, their head high, their mouth slightly open, and their tongue exposed, loose stance, with their weight equal on all feet, and their tail down and relaxed. This dog is content and relaxed. This dog is not worried about a threat and is not concerned about anything. No matter if they looked relaxed, you should approach the dog with caution and don't try to rush a dog into greeting you, even if they are relaxed.

2. Alert and checking things out

This type of dog has the ears forward (may twitch), eyes are wide, the mouth is closed, smoother forehead and nose, slightly leaning forwards, the tail is horizontal, and it may move a bit from side to side. If your dog has detected something they don't know or find interesting, these could signal that he is on alert and paying attention while also assessing things to see if there is a threat.

3. Happy dog

A happy dog is easily spotted because it will seem loose all over. They shouldn't be holding any tension in their muscles or mouth, and their eyes should be relaxed and a bit squinty. The most common signs of a happy and relaxed dog are the mouth is slightly open, the ears are neutral, the eyes are soft, and sometimes the tail will loosely wag. The looseness in their body echoes the loose and relaxed feeling that the dog has about the interaction that is going on. You could also know that they slightly lower their ears and head, and they might even lay down and rollover.

4. Dominant aggressive

A dominantly aggressive dog with have their hackles raised, ears forward and spread, forehead could be wrinkled, nose wrinkled, lips curled, teeth visible, mouth open and C-shaped, stiff-legged stance, leaning slightly forward, tail raised and bristled, and the tail is stiff with small movements. A dominantly aggressive dog is showing that he is socially dominant and is showing aggression if he were to be challenged. Knowing if your dog is submissive or dominant can help the relationship and can help you be more aware of how other dogs are acting around you.

5. Fearful

When they are scared, dogs could lean away, cower, or try to hide under or behind something, which are all signs that they want to avoid the dog or person who is coming towards them. It's important that you pay attention to your dog's eyes for any sign of fear. This is where half-moon or whale eyes come into play. This lets you know that he has his head turned a bit away from what he is afraid of, but their eyes are still looking at it. Some other common signs of fear are holding perfectly still, yawning when not tired, lighting up their paw, averting eye contact, and lip licking. All of these signs coincide with submissive behaviors. Knowing how to spot fear in a dog is helpful when it comes to spotting aggression because aggression and fear tend to go hand in hand.

6. Fearful and aggressive

This type of dog will have a lowered body, hackles raise, ears back, pupils dilated, nose wrinkled, lips slightly curled, corner of the mouth pulled back, and tail tucked. While this dog may be frightened, it is not a submissive dog and could attack if pressed. A dog typically gives you these signs when they are faced with an individual who they pose as a threat to them.

When it comes to aggression, the transition from fear to aggression starts with a direct start into eyes fully open. When it comes to confrontation behavior, this is seen not only in dogs but throughout other species. This stare lets you know that there is something amiss, and all other signs that come after this indicate an increase in aggression. Unlike the looseness of a happy dog, aggressive dogs will be stiff. The stiffness helps them look taller.

With dogs, a vertical tail shows a high social order rank. They could be experiencing piloerection. This erection is closely linked to their nervous system. It will occur whenever they are super-aroused, and we tend to see it whenever they are feeling extra-fearful or aggressive. If your dog is showing any signs of aggression, you should speak with a vet behaviorist or a trainer for advice on how to de-escalate or put a stop to aggressive behavior. This could mean that you have to remove triggers of aggression or fear, helping them socialize with others, and behavior modification.

7. Distressed and stressed

This type of dog has dilated pupils, ears back, body lowered, tail down, sweating through pads, and rapid panting with the mouth corners back. This dog is likely feeling stressed by something around them. These signals are normally just a broadcast of his state of mind and aren't being shown towards any particular person.

8. Worried and fearful

You might notice that this dog leaves behind sweaty footprints, their tail is down, and it might be wagging a bit, their ears are back, body lowered, forehead smooth, brief eye contact licks at the face of the dominant dog or in the air, corners of the mouth are back, and paw raised. This dog is letting you know that they are submissive or fearful. All of these signs are designed to pacify the person they see as of higher social status or a dog they think is a potential threat so that they don't have to face any other challenges. If they are showing these signs, they might not feel comfortable where they are.

9. Extreme fear or total submission

For this dog, they might sprinkle some urine, the tail is tucked, rolls onto back, ears back and flat, head turned to avoid eye contact, smooth nose and forehead, eyes partly closed, and the corners of the mouth will be pulled back. This position is indicating complete submission. They are trying to let you know that they accept their lower status by groveling before a threatening or higher-ranking individual in the hopes that they can avoid a physical confrontation.

10. Playfulness

This dog will have their tail up in a broad wave, pupils dilated, ears up, front end lowers, and mouth open with the tongue hanging out. This is normally only held for a moment before they run after something. This is a simple invitation to play. It could be accompanied by an excited bark or a playful attack and retreat.

This is the body language that everybody wants to see. Like the play itself, playful body language is silly and fun. The dog could appear bouncy, and they could be exhibiting similar body language cues that they do when they are happy. Mainly, you should see fast and free movements, and they may even bark or growl, which will be different from the aggressive forms.

No one body signal will act along. They all work together as a type of package. When it comes to reading your dog's communication, you need to take a look at every single they are using, from eye shape to tail height. They are essentially "talking" to you all of the time. Plus, with this newfound understanding of their emotions, you can better predict their behavior and prevent problems.

When it comes to learning your dog's body language, it is similar to learn sign language. It gives you the chance to communicate with your dog and understand them better. One of the best ways to figure out how your dog is feeling is to pay attention to their body language. It allows you to respond in an appropriate manner in any given situation. You will know if they are scared or when you need to defuse the confrontation. This is going to result in a stronger relationship with your pooch.

There is a caveat to mastering canine body language. You have to look at the body language in context. Only you can understand your dog's history and all of its quirks. You need to pay attention to everything else that is going on around your dog. If they are licking their lips for a treat, then they likely aren't anxious. Your dog could yawn because they are tired and ready for bed, and not because they are scared. But if you see them staring intently at a dog, they don't know, standing stiff and showing their teeth? You are going to want to be on standby for that.

Chapter 8: General Puppy Care

Puppies have to be the most adorable thing in the world. The happiest times of my life have been when I had a cute, cuddly puppy. These are the most memorable times for your whole family, and everybody can help care for and love your puppy. But parenting a new puppy can be difficult. It is definitely no walk in the park. This chapter will help you take care of the newest addition to your family.

When it comes time to bring your puppy home, you can count on three things: huge adjustment to your lifestyle, cleaning up numerous accidents, and unlimited joy. As you will learn, a puppy needs a lot more than just food and water to thrive. It might be hard work at first, but it will be worth the effort in the long run. Creating healthy habits in those first few weeks will build a foundation for many years of happiness for both your puppy and you.

- Finding a Vet

The first place you need to take your puppy is to the vet for a checkup. This visit will help make sure your puppy doesn't have any huge health problems, is healthy, doesn't have any birth defects, etc. this can help you take those first necessary steps toward creating a good health routine. If you don't have a vet yet, ask family members or friends who have pets where they take theirs. If you rescued your puppy from a shelter, ask for their recommendations as they usually have certain vets that they use.

- Picking Out The Right Puppy

If you know the time is right for you to get a puppy, you now have the task of choosing the best one. Maybe your new puppy will find you. Puppies might come to you by chance. You might feel instantly connected to them, and you just know in your soul that this one is the perfect one for you. This doesn't always happen. You might have to go out and find the right one for you.

First, you need to look at your life and think about what you are looking for. Do you want a mixed breed, purebred, large, small, etc.? There are other things you need to think about, too, like their exercise needs, grooming needs, possible health problems, and temperament.

Next, you will have to figure out where to find this new puppy. Are you going to go to a shelter to find your puppy? Maybe you know a respectable breeder. You need to have lots of patience and do a lot of research during this part of the process. Once you have found the perfect puppy, you are going to have a best friend for life.

- What Will You Name Your Puppy?

When a new puppy comes into your family, you now have the job of naming this new member. You will be using this name for the rest of the dog's life, so you need to make a good choice here.

Choose something that sounds nice but isn't too long. It needs to be simple and easy to say so your puppy can understand it. It is important not to name your dog something that sounds like commands or other things you plan on teaching them.

You could name the puppy something that helps to describe its appearance or personality. You might want to pick something that is unique. After you have picked a name, use it a lot. It won't be long before your puppy has learned its name and will respond to it.

- Get The Most Out Of Your First Visit

At this initial visit, your vet will do a thorough physical and get some information from you so they can have a complete history of your puppy's health. This is your chance to get all the important information you need to know so you can be a loving, responsible, and informed pet parent. You will probably spend about one hour with the vet. You will also need to bring everyone who lives with you to this appointment too. Here are some topics that you will need to talk about in this first visit:

1. The puppy's diet – how much and how often to feed
2. Potty training the puppy
3. Obedience training
4. Behavior training
5. Neutering or spaying
6. Any signs of sickness
7. Options for finding and treating any parasites
8. Vaccination schedule

Most of these will be the same for every puppy; your vet will take into consideration factors like lifestyle, age, and breed of your dog plus any behavioral or current health problems so they can make any recommendation that can be suited just for your puppy.

- Find Good Food

Knowing puppy food is a big part of being a responsible pet parent. Your puppy is growing in ways that can impact their quality of life for several years, and this is why you need to find food that has been formulated for puppies rather than just buying the cheapest adult dog food. Look on the bag's label to see if you can find a statement from the AAFCO to make sure the food you pick is going to be the best for your puppy. This will help you make sure that the food you choose will meet or even exceed the nutritional requirements for your puppy.

Their diet makes a difference in your puppy's well-being and health. Before you decide on food, do some research. Keep in mind that if the food you first pick out doesn't meet your expectations, you can slowly switch them to another food.

Today, your choice of food seems endless. There are some pet owners who like to feed their puppy premium food, while other people think natural or holistic diets would be better. Raw and homemade diets are also getting more popular.

While you are researching your puppy's food, think about the ingredients, nutrients, and taste. Be sure you choose food that will be good for your puppy's growth. Never buy "maintenance" or adult food for your puppy. Their food needs to be healthy for them, and they need to enjoy eating it.

Small or medium-sized breeds could move to adult food by the age of nine months. Larger breeds need to be fed puppy food until they are between one and two years old. Be sure your puppy has fresh water at all times, especially early in the day, as this helps them break down the food they eat during the day. This also helps keep them well hydrated. You will need to feed them throughout the day:

1. Between six and 12 weeks of age, feed them four times each day
2. Between three and six months, feed them three times each day
3. Between six and 12 months, feed them twice each day

You will also need to create a walking and feeding schedule as it can help you with housetraining your puppy. Puppies can learn, understand, and they actually have structure to their day. Make sure you follow the vets' recommended feeding schedule. Talk to your vet about this and ask for their advice to make sure you are feeding your puppy right.

You should never share your food with your puppy. They love begging for what you eat, and you might be tempted to give them a tiny amount of what you are eating. This isn't dangerous, but it will be a hard habit to break because they will think that they will be able to share your food every time.

You need to stick with your puppy's feeding schedule plus a good diet. Start training your puppy early on ways they should behave while you eat. This could involve putting them outside or putting them in their crate until they learn the right behavior.

- Keep Your Pup Healthy

Take some treats with you so you can reinforce their good behaviors when they are in the vet's office. Take all the steps needed to make it a fun experience so your puppy won't be scared of the vet.

During the puppy's first six months, they will be seeing the vet a lot. This will start with their vaccines and will normally lead to either neutering or spaying. Puppies will need to be neutered or spayed by six months of age.

Your vet will be able to find any possible health problems early, and they can advise you about how to care for your puppy for a long, long time. The first visit will open the door of communication between the vet and you. In order to keep expenses down, you might want to buy insurance for your pet that will cover about 80 percent of their health care costs.

- Signs of Illness

Puppies are very susceptible to diseases and illnesses that might be extremely serious, and most of these are completely preventable. This is the main reason vaccines are very important. Puppy vaccines won't keep your puppy healthy from all illnesses. The best way to prevent illnesses is by diligently monitoring your puppy's symptoms and behavior.

If you see any of these symptoms, you need to call your vet right away:

1. Not able to poop or pee
2. Discharge coming from their nose
3. Discharge coming from their eyes
4. Red or swollen eyes
5. Pale gums
6. Coughing or wheezing
7. Problems breathing
8. Diarrhea
9. Lethargy
10. Sore or swollen belly
11. Vomiting
12. Not gaining any weight
13. No appetite

All of these symptoms show an emergency situation, and you need to take them to the vet immediately. If you do see any of the above, call your vet immediately.

- Puppy Vaccines

Vaccines will protect your puppy and other animals from fatal illnesses. Kittens and puppies are just like human babies, and they all need basic vaccines to take over when their antibodies fade. Puppy vaccines are the most important aspect of their life.

The bad news is that vaccinating your pet has become very controversial for people who are afraid of vaccines. This is why most vets are going for a three-year vaccine instead of the normal yearly one for dogs. When talking about puppies, they have a completely different set of rules since the threat of diseases is very high in dogs. Your puppy might die from these diseases, and some might even be spread to humans.

Getting regular vaccines lets your vet's office see your puppy every few weeks while monitoring its health and growth. Ask your vet what the best plan for vaccines would be for your baby.

Puppy vaccines normally happen every three to four weeks until they reach about 16 weeks old. They will continue getting booster during adulthood. There are non-core and core vaccines that your puppy can get, and your vet can help you figure out which ones your puppy is going to need. A normal vaccine schedule might look like this:

1. Six to ten weeks, they will get the kennel cough and DHPP
2. 11 to 14 weeks, they will get canine influenza, leptospirosis, and DHPP
3. 15 to 16 weeks, they will get rabies, canine influenza, leptospirosis, and DHPP

You need to make sure our puppy stays current with their vaccines. These have been proven to fight against many preventable illnesses and diseases that could happen without the right immunizations. Puppy vaccines are a big responsibility when taking care of a puppy. Your puppy doesn't deserve anything less than having the chance to be happy and healthy their entire life.

- Make Sure To Bond With Puppy

The bond you create with your puppy starts the very moment they come into your life, and this will never quit growing. This bond can be nurtured by participating in different activities, general exercise, playtime, grooming, training, and affection. You could also take them to an obedience class. You can begin training them in sports such as flyball or agility or even getting them into shows.

The best way to bond with your dog is to let your dog bond with other people, plus getting involved with animal-assisted therapy. If your puppy gets chosen as a therapy animal, you can train them to visit people in nursing homes and hospitals. Preserving and strengthening the bond between humans and canine has many health benefits for both of you.

- Dealing With a Teething Puppy

Yes, puppies teethe just like babies teethe. Yes, it can be painful and annoying at times. You need to know that teething is another natural part of your puppy's maturity and growth process. This behavior could get out of hand if you don't give them the right outlets during this phase.

Puppies, just like most babies, aren't born with teeth. Deciduous teeth will start to appear in three weeks. By the time the puppy is between six and eight weeks old, it should have a full set of 28 teeth. When a puppy is teething, they might target any object to chew and gnaw on to relieve some of the discomforts that are associated with teething. Teething is essential for puppies for these reasons:

1. Teething is a defense mechanism
2. Teething is a way to get attention
3. Nipping and biting is part of the canine culture

You need to give your puppy the right teething toys and devices according to their age. You need to gently reinforce that biting and nipping other animals, furniture, and people isn't allowed. If you have other pets during teething time, they will help keep the puppy from getting too out of control. Make sure you monitor the playtime between pets to make sure that innocent teething doesn't turn into something a lot more serious.

- When To Neuter or Spay Your Puppy

Neutering and spaying should be done between five and six months of age. There are some breeds that recommend waiting longer to prevent specific cancers. Your vet will look at all this information when you have your first visit and will talk about it with you. They will help you make all the right decisions for your puppy.

Most vets support early neutering and spaying. If you delay this process past their sexual maturity could cause mammary tumors in female dogs or testicular cancer in males. Basically, a puppy can recover faster than adults can. This means it will be an easier surgery, and it could reduce diseases later in life. I love puppies and animals of any kind, but I also think that there are too many who wind up in shelters or killed because the pet population can't be controlled.

Chapter 9: Socializing

Socializing a puppy will help make sure you have a well-adjusted, confident, and happy puppy. The world belongs to your puppy, and we are just allowed to live in it. This doesn't mean your puppy gets a pass on being polite. Be sure your puppy becomes an upstanding citizen by following these simple steps.

- When Should You Socialize Your Puppy

In the first three months of your puppy's life, they are going to experience some periods of socialization that will share their personality permanently and the way they react to their environment once they are grown. Exposing them to various situations, places, and people slowly and gently now will make a big difference to their temperament.

Anytime you purchase a puppy from a breeder who is responsible, this process needs to begin before you bring them home. The breeder needs to gently handle them in the first few weeks of their life to help them become confident and friendly puppies. By the age of three weeks, puppies might start approaching a person who is looking at them. Having a good breeder who encourages the puppy and people to have positive experiences together can shape the puppy's behavior as an adult. When their puppies start growing, a good breeder will let them experience safe outside and inside environments, gentle handling, smells, sounds, crates, and car rides.

- Why Do You Need To Socialize Your Puppy

The main idea about socializing your puppy is you would like to help them become accustomed to various smells, sounds, and sights in a good way. Having the right socialization could keep a dog from being afraid around children, riding in a car, and it can help them turn into a happy, well-mannered companion.

A puppy who is confident and well adjusted might even save their life one day. Not socializing your puppy the right way might cause behavior problems in their life later. "Behavioral problems and not infectious diseases are the main cause of death in dogs under the age of three years. Begin taking your dog into public places when your vet says it is safe; they will learn how to behave in different situations while enjoying interacting with others.

- How Can You Socialize The Puppy

As I mentioned above, the breeder should begin this process as early as a few days after they are born. They will handle them gently and let them explore their surroundings. Once you get the puppy home, the critical period of socialization will continue. It is your job to keep this process moving forward. Here are some steps you can do:

1. Make sure they have their vaccines

In order to keep your puppy from getting sick, you should never expose them to public places or other animals until they have had their vaccinations. It would be a great idea to find a vet before you even bring your baby home. A normal vaccination schedule starts at about six weeks old and will continue every three to four weeks until they have received all their shots. After that, they will get a booster once a year or as your vet prescribes.

The main vaccines your puppy needs are rabies, canine hepatitis, distemper, and canine parvovirus. These get their bodies ready to fight off any contagious diseases. They absolutely need these immunizations. Other vaccines might be given based on their risk exposure, like where you live. Some of these vaccines might be Lyme disease, leptospirosis, canine influenza, and Bordetella. Your vet will help you figure out which of these vaccines your puppy might need.

2. Introduce your puppy to new smells, sounds, and sights

The entire world is unusual, strange, and new to them, so you have to think of all the things they encounter as a chance to make new associations in a positive way. Try to find different textures, noises, places, and people where you can expose your puppy to these sensations. This means to make him walk on linoleum, tile, hardwood, and carpeted floors. Let him meet people who use a cane, walker or are in a wheelchair. People wearing hoodies, children carrying an umbrella, wearing sunglasses, or has a beard. Think of this as a scavenger hunt. Get out and explore with your puppy.

3. Involve the whole family

When you get different people to take part in your puppy's socialization, you will constantly be getting them out of their comfort zone. Show them that they might experience new things no matter who they are with. Create a fun game for the children by getting them to write down a list of all the new things that the puppy encountered on the day they spent with them, like "the puppy heard a fire truck siren," "met a person wearing a baseball cap," or "they met the man driving the ice cream truck."

4. Play some socialization games

These games are a great way to teach your puppy how great it could feel to meet new people and get petted by them. Giving them treats to encourage them can help their progress. Remember to look at the recommended feeding guidelines to make sure you don't give them too many treats in a day.

If you have a group of friends, you could play a game called "pass the puppy." This is the way you play:

Make sure everybody has some treats. One person will pick up the puppy and hold them the right way. Make sure they are supporting their rear end. Every time the puppy lets a person touch their tail, ear, or paw, give them a treat. The puppy is then passed to the next person, and the routine gets repeated.

Another game to play is done where everybody is sitting in a circle. You put the puppy in the center, and then one person calls to the puppy to "come" to them. They will be holding a small treat. When the puppy goes to them, they will give the puppy lots of praise and a treat. Another person will now do the same thing.

5. Make the experience positive

The most important thing to remember when you are introducing your puppy to all these new things that they are getting lots of praise and treats. This will help them associate what they are being exposed to, and feeling like new experiences are fun. Remember to break their treats into small pieces that will be easy for them to digest. Never get anxious when doing this with your puppy because they can read our emotions. If you are nervous when you introduce your puppy to another dog, they are going to feel nervous, too. They might be afraid of other dogs for the rest of their lives.

6. Take it slow

Don't try to do too much too quickly. If you would like your puppy to get used to being handled by various people that they don't know, begin with some family member and slowly bring in one person they don't know, then introduce them to two, etc. If you start this process by taking your new puppy to a big party or an extremely public place, it might be too overwhelming for them and cause them to be afraid of strangers in their future.

7. Take them to classes

After your puppy has gotten their vaccinations, you can begin taking them to puppy classes. These classes can help your puppy start understanding their basic commands. The best advantage is they get exposed to other people and dogs. Good trainers will mediate all the meetings, so the people and dogs are happy and safe throughout the process. You should be able to find these classes through your local community center or vet.

8. Go public

After your puppy has gotten used to some stimuli, get them outside of their comfort zone so you can expand the number of experiences they get. Take them to a pet store, to a friend's house, walk them on a new street, etc. After they have gotten all of their puppy vaccinations, wait for a little over one week before you take them to a dog park. Make sure you follow the park's safety procedures.

9. Help them earn their STAR

You can show off their hard work by allowing them to earn their first AKC title of STAR. This stands for socialization, training, activity, and responsible. Once they have finished their six-week training class, they will take a test that is done by an evaluator who has been approved by the AKC. They will get tested on letting someone hold them, tolerating a harness or collar, letting people pet them, etc. You, as their owner, have to take a pledge to be responsible for their entire life. This program is open to any mixed-breed or purebred dog that is under a year old.

- What If You Have An Older Dog

All this information about socializing your puppy brings up another question: "What about older dogs?" If you have adopted an older dog from a shelter, you could still help them associate scary or new situations with positive experiences, even if you missed the critical puppy stage. You can slowly introduce your adult dog to new sounds, smells, and sights by carefully supervising them. Remember to give them praise and treats, too, while they are overcoming their hesitation and fears. If they are extremely scared, they might need to be treated by a vet or animal behaviorist.

Socializing Them With Humans

Even though you might be taking your puppy out for walks and in public places can help them get used to the people and world around them. Meeting the mailman and hearing cars pass by them on the road is going to be a bit scary at first, but after a few trips, they will get used to these sounds and sights.

Keep your baby on a leash while you get some exercise. There will be a lot to see and lots and lots of smells. Take various routes and let your puppy have a chance to meet new friends and experience all kinds of sights and sounds.

- Change Up Your Routine

You have to expose your puppy to various people like children, women, and men so that they can get used to having people around them that are a lot bigger than them. This idea comes from the fact that if your puppy just hangs out with you, they might get scared of anybody who isn't you. It is critical to change up your puppy's social calendar. You have to take some time for some meet and greets for your puppy.

1. Get a pet sitter or hire a dog walker to expose your puppy to various caregivers throughout the day.
2. Remember the basics. A puppy that is confident with its routine and training will grow up to be a well-rounded adult dog.

3. Give your puppy treats so they can associate new experiences and people as being positive things.
4. If anybody wants to pet your puppy, make sure they keep their hands where the puppy can see them, like on their chin or chest.

- Socialize At The Right Time

Between the ages of three and 12 weeks old, this is the puppy's sweet spot for socialization. You need to expose your new puppy to:

1. Other dogs
2. Cats
3. Objects in their neighborhood like benches, skateboards, strollers, bicycles, street signs, etc
4. Vehicles
5. Beaches
6. Woods
7. Water
8. Parks
9. Urban environments
10. People handling various parts of their body like tail, paws, ears, etc
11. Unfamiliar clothing like hats, sunglasses, jackets, and hoods
12. People they don't know

Once they are over 18 weeks, it will be harder to socialize them, but it isn't completely impossible. Don't worry if you have an older dog; old dogs can be taught new tricks.

- Training Classes

Some puppy boot camp hasn't ever hurt anybody or puppy. To find one near you, you could call your vet or your community center. These are great places where you can meet new people and dogs in a controlled and safe environment.

Socializing Your Dog With New Dogs

- Get Lots of Treats

Man dogs will do anything for treats, so it would be great to have lots of these on hand to keep them on their best behavior. If your dog has a great interaction with other dogs, what are you going to do? You give them praise and a treat. This will encourage them to have positive social behaviors.

Tasty treats will get you more mileage from your dog. You will be able to find which ones your dog likes the best. Pieces of hardboiled eggs, small bites of cooked chicken, or string cheese are very popular with a puppy. You might need to adjust their calorie intake during meals to accommodate the extra calories during snack time.

- Go To A Pet Shop

Take your waggy-tailed puppy to the park and let them make their rounds. If they are good at recall, you can try taking them to an off-leash park. You could also create a date to take your puppy to a friend's house that has a dog.

If you don't have compostable poop bags or a shampoo that smells good, take your dog to the store so they can see what is going on. They might make a new acquaintance. You might also meet other people who have dogs in your neighborhood, and you could make new friends, too, and this could set a stage for more playdates for both of you.

- Watch The Cues Coming From Your Dog

Be sure that every interaction is long enough so they can get acquainted but not too long, so your puppy gets too tired. This is just like you are your best friend; if you spend too much time with each other, you may begin noticing things that you hadn't ever seen before.

- Use Caution

Introducing a Great Dane to a Chihuahua might sound cute, but you have to use cautions when you are introducing two different breeds of dogs. Make sure the other dog is friendly before you create a meet and sniff. You need to know the signs of being discomfort with your puppy, like a tail between their legs, yawning, or panting. If you see these signs, you need to act accordingly.

Chapter 10: Puppy Training Mistakes

Getting a new puppy is exciting. If you don't know the basic "do's" and "don'ts" of training your puppy, things can take a turn for the worse very quickly. You are doing the right things since you are trying to train your puppy. Potty training problems, constantly chewing on everything, incessant barking, and other "bad" behaviors could change all those great feelings into regret and frustration. Don't allow a minor mistake to get in your way. Although they are insignificant, it might surprise you to learn that some things could slow down your training progress. If you can stay away from these common mistakes, you will increase your chances of enjoying your new puppy and mentoring them into adulthood.

Here are some mistakes you need to stay away from:

- Taking Them From Mom Too Soon

This is probably the biggest mistake people make. In the first eight weeks of a dog's life, they are getting lots of nurturing from mom, and they are learning valuable social skills from their siblings. There are some shelters and breeders who take the puppies away from their mom and siblings way too soon. This cuts short the social imprinting process, and it could cause some problems. If the puppy leaves the litter too soon, they usually have problems learning not to bite, and they won't know how to interact the right way with people and other dogs. They could also get skittish toward people they don't know and other animals. Stay away from these problems that can last their entire life by just waiting until your puppy is older than eight weeks to take them away from their siblings and mom.

- Waiting Too Long

You need to start training your puppy the minute you get them home. It doesn't matter how old they are either. Don't try to wait until they get a bit older because, by this time, they have probably begun developing bad habits. Training your dog isn't the same as "behavior management." With training, your goal is to shape the puppy's behavior to teach them ways to respond to certain phrases.

Puppies that are too young may not be ready to learn some advanced commands, but you still need to begin working on basic commands and house training. With time, you are going to create deeper bonds with your dog. They are going to get accustomed to your routines as they mature. You can then try some more fun things such as tricks. You can then try some advanced training or tricks.

- You Run Back Inside After The Puppy Pees or Poops

Puppies love being outside and want to explore their area; it isn't going to take them long to learn that after they pee or poop, all their fun is over. Because of this, you might have a dog who will not go to the bathroom outside until they can't hold it anymore. This could cause problems for those times when you are in a hurry, and you need them to go potty fast. What you need to be doing is taking your puppy outside on a leash while waiting patiently until they have done their business. When they have finished, give them praise and a reward and then take them for a short walk or play with them for a bit. By doing this, they are going to learn how to potty and will go as soon as you take them outside.

- Not Beginning Training Quickly Enough

By the time a puppy is eight weeks old, they are old enough to learn basic commands when they walk into your house. Most people don't realize this, and the thing that the only training that they should do is housebreak them. This is so not true. By starting some simple commands like come, stay, down, and sit, you are going to give them a head start while creating some enthusiasm and focus that is critical to having a well-mannered puppy. Begin training them on the first day you get them.

- Not Enough Training

Training your puppy isn't something that you do once and never again. You are going to get better results if you regularly train your dog even after they have mastered a cue or action. Choose one thing that you want to work on and do short training sessions two or three times each week. Find some fun things you can teach your dog but go back to the basics every now and then.

Your dog will never be through with training. You need to always be teaching your dog something as they get older. Continuous training will keep their skills sharpened. Training is fun for your dog and is a great way for you to bond with them.

- Allowing Your Dog To Give "Love Nibbles"

Puppies are going to use their teeth to explore just like a toddler will use their hands. You can expect them to put their mouth and teeth on everything anytime they get excited. Allowing them to give you nips when you are playing with them might seem harmless, but this isn't something you want your dog to do once they are grown. If you have already let your puppy do this you can try to redirect them to a toy when they begin biting you. When they tug on the right toy give them praise and reward them by playing with them. Puppies grow extremely fast so play as much as you can with them.

- Not Crate Training Them

Dogs are natural denning animals and they love having snug spots where they can nest or eat. Crates take advantage of their natural desire to not soil where they eat or sleep. A crate is the best place to feed your puppy because they will be able to eat by themselves away from people or other pets you might have. Choose a crate that is appropriate for your breed of dog. It needs to be tall enough so your puppy can stand up in it and long enough so they can turn around inside. If the crate is too big, they might use the bathroom in one part of it and sleep in the other. Feed them inside the crate and get them to sleep in it, too. If you can't be with them all the time, they need to be in their crate or have a puppy sitter. Even though they can sleep in the crate during the night, it is best not to make them stay in the crate no more than six hours overnight or four hours in the daytime.

- Using a "One-Size-Fits-All" Training

Don't get the first dog training book you see and read it and then think that is all you have to do. Don't just talk to one friend who has dogs either. There are several successful programs and styles of dog training and there won't be two dogs who are the same. Sometime you might need to talk to several people and use all the information you have collected to create a training program that works for you and your dog.

Try out different things and see which ones work the best for your dog. Combine various types of training to make a plan that will fit your dog and you. You could even try some different training classes. Never give up to fast, but never be afraid to change if things aren't working out for you.

- You Get Too Excited When Your Doorbell Rings

It is great to share in the excitement of having a pizza delivered or friends coming to your house. You are psyching up your puppy when you rush to the door or you ask them:

"Who's at the door?" This could cause some bad habits such as jumping on guests, running to the door, or your puppy running out the door and into the streets. Keep your greeting low-key from the start and train your puppy ways to be nice when you have visitors. You could put them on a leash if you know you are having people over and give them praise and rewards when they stay at your side without jumping on others. You could train them to get in their crate when to doorbell rings and then give them praise and a treat for staying there until you call them.

- Letting Them Be Too Independent

Puppies are going to be curious about their surroundings. If you let your puppy wander around your home without supervision, they are going to get into some kind of trouble. They could begin chewing on shoes, clothing, loose wires, going potty inside, or finding a way to get outside and possibly getting hurt. Most "accidents" that happen in the home is caused by not being supervised well and is going to cause delays in getting them housetrained. You can prevent this by making sure that your new puppy is in their crate, with you, or inside a fenced in yard. When they are inside you can try keeping their leash tethered to your belt so they can go with you when inside. This shows them where they are allowed to go. Once their housetraining is done and they don't have any more accidents, you can slowly start increasing their independence when inside.

- Being Inconsistent

You have to keep your responses to your dog consistent when you are training them. If you don't, you are only confusing your puppy. You might find that you have accidentally reinforced some bad behaviors.

Look at this example: you have made a rule that the puppy can't get on the couch. You are feeling down one day and want to have some cuddle time with them. You let the get on the couch with you to help you feel better. The next day you fuss at them for jumping up on the couch, they aren't going to understand why they can't be with you today but got to cuddle with you yesterday.

Begging would be another example of this kind of mistake. If you never give your puppy any of the food you are eating, they aren't going to get into the habit of begging for food when you eat. They might try it a couple of times, but ignoring them or telling them to lay down is going to discourage this behavior. If somebody does give him some food, they will associate begging as a reward and they will continue to beg.

One more example would be rewarding your dog any time they "sort of" does a command right. If you are trying to train your puppy to lie down, you only give them a reward when their entire body is on the floor. If you were to give them a reward BEFORE they entire body is down, this is being inconsistent. When you tell them to "lie down," they might get confused and keep doing it wrong.

- Pulling While Leash Training

Puppies are going to do what will work for them. If you let your puppy pull when you are leash training them, they are going to do it forever, even when they are a BIG dog. Going for walks with your puppy aren't going to be any fun plus you might be hurting your back and shoulders in the process. Teach your puppy from the beginning that keeping their leash loose will get them praise, treats, and fun walks. Anytime the pulling begins, stop walking. When you stat consistent, they are going to learn the right way to walk rather than trying to be a bulldozer and pulling you forward.

- Keeping Food Out At All Times

Leaving food out all day is a huge mistake. When you let them eat all day long, you are lessening your chances of creating a potty schedule. If they always have food in their belly, they are going to need to go to the potty more often. When you feed them at a certain time each day, you will be "synchronizing" their system. This is going to make housetraining them easier, too. Feeding at certain times will create a better food drive with your puppy. Being able to predict when they are hungry is a wonderful training tool. About 20 minutes before their meal, they are going to do anything to a treat. Feeding at specific times will let you know exactly the amount of food they are eating. By doing this you will be able to keep them at a perfect weight. People who free feed their puppies don't ever know exactly how much food they are eating because you are adding to their dish during the day.

- Harsh Discipline

Most dog trainers today will agree than pusinshing your puppy during training is not effective at all. Basically, dogs will perform better for a reward through positivity. Using mild aversions like shaking a rattle can or spray bottle of water could help you in certain situations and don't cause the puppy any harm. Other things might cause a very dangerous situation. Harsh discipline are any actions like jerking their leash, grabbing them by the scruff of their neck, staring them down, alpha rolls, hitting them, or yelling at them. Every one of these actions has bad consequences like:

1. Provoking aggressive reaction from your puppy that puts you or others in danger
2. Could make your dog scared of you
3. You might hurt your puppy

If you really think that harsh discipline is needed so you can become dominant to your dog, they you are doing everything wrong. Thinking that humans are "pack leaders" is a very outdated concept and come from inaccurate research about wolves and dogs. You need to do some research and learn ways you can earn your dog's respect. Their training process needs to be fun for them and you. It is a great way for you to create a closer bond with your dog. It should never be about bullying them into submission.

- Rubbing Their Nose In Their Accidents

A puppy who is only ten weeks old doesn't know what you are teaching her when you shove their nose into their poop. The only thing you are showing them is that you get mad when they poop. This only teaches them to be scared of their poop. This could make them poop in spots where you can't see it like in a closet or behind furniture. If you crate train them the right way, you will not have this problem. If you catch them going poop inside, clap a few times and say "aah-ahh" and get them outside as fast as you can. When they do go outside, remember to reward them. If they did poop inside, make sure you clean it well with an enzyme cleaner.

- Making Your Dog "Come" For Doing Something Bad

Would you want to have to go to someone if you knew you were going to be punished, yelled at, or have something bad happen? No, you wouldn't. Your dog doesn't want to either. Each time you call your dog to you so you can punish them, you are actually punishing them for coming to you. This is going to discourage them from coming to you when you call them. Getting them to come to you is the most important thing you can train your dog to do. You can't ruin this by making this stupid mistake.

If you absolutely have to do things that you dog doesn't like such as trimming their nails or taking a bath, just go get them rather than calling them to you. If you do get angry, you need to calm yourself down before you give them a command. Keep in mind that your dog won't learn anything from being yelled at or punished after they have done the undesired behavior.

Conclusion

Thanks for reading all the way through the book. I hope that you have found everything informative and helpful. Welcoming a new puppy into your life can be a wonderful and exciting experience. However, it can get overwhelming with the number of things you need to do.

With this book, you should have the information you need to help get your puppy established in their new home, housebroken, and happy. Puppies are a big ball of enjoy, so you can't expect all of this to work overnight. Give them time, and give yourself time. If something doesn't seem to be working just right, try doing it a different way. Eventually everything will come together. You will find that you can read your dog without any problems, and you won't be cleaning up pee out of the floor forever.

Lastly, I would like to ask that if you have found any part of this book helpful, a review on Amazon is always appreciated.

Printed in Dunstable, United Kingdom